CIMA: Pass First Time!

PUBLISHING

David R. Harris

(Illustrated by 'Sully')

ELSEVIER

AMSTERDAM • BOSTON • HEIDELBERG • LONDON • NEW YORK • OXFORD
PARIS • SAN DIEGO • SAN FRANCISCO • SINGAPORE • SYDNEY • TOKYO

CIMA Publishing
An imprint of Elsevier
Linacre House, Jordan Hill, Oxford OX2 8DP
30, Corporate Drive, Burlington, MA 01803

First Published 2007

British Library Cataloguing in Publication Data
A catalogue record for this book is available from the British Library

Library of Congress Cataloguing in Publication Data
A catalogue record for this book is available from the Library of Congress

ISBN 10: 0-7506-8396-1
ISBN 13: 978-0-7506-8396-8

For information on all Elsevier publications visit our website at http://books.elsevier.com

Printed and bound in Great Britain by MPG Books Ltd. Bodmin Cornwall

Contents

GETTING YOUR FRIENDS AND FAMILY TO GIVE YOU SUPPORT IS REALLY IMPORTANT.

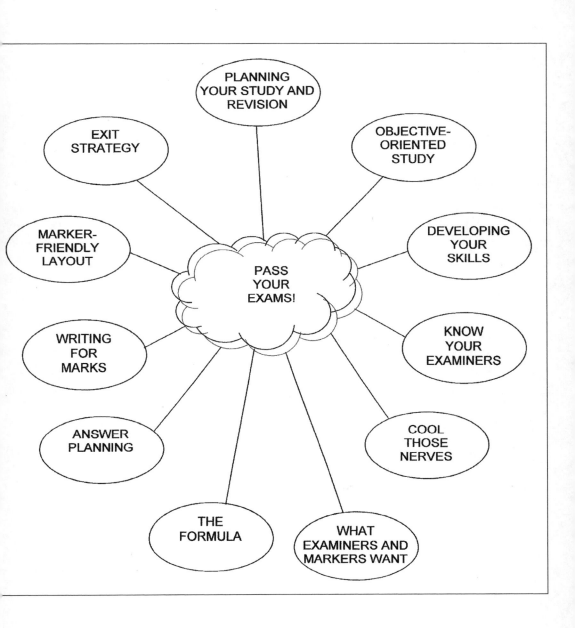

Background to this text, and how to use it 1

1 Background to this text, and how to use it

Why write a book about study and exam techniques? Because they are really important!

From my many years of experience as a lecturer, marker, and examiner for a leading accountancy professional body, I've learnt just how important exam technique can be to students. Many well-prepared candidates sit exams, every year, and fail them because their exam technique is poor. At the same time, quite a few average students pass because they have good exam technique.

Developing good exam technique isn't cheating. It's simply a way of making sure that you get all the marks you deserve. Most of the advice in this book is just about maximising your potential, and many of the ideas will also improve your report–writing and communication skills in the workplace.

This isn't really a textbook, more of a collection of tips and hints to help you be successful in exams. If you want to read this book from cover to cover, please do. If you want to 'dip in' to the sections as they become relevant to your studies, that's fine too. Alternatively, you might just flick through the book, looking at Sully's excellent illustrations.

At the end of each chapter, you'll find a 'mind map' of the main points. You might, when you've read the book, photocopy these mind maps and carry them around as 'revision notes'. Alternatively, you could always enlarge them and stick them to your walls. You think I'm joking? Read on...

On a slightly more serious note, as a CIMA marker and examiner myself I know what you need to do in order to pass. If you follow my advice I can't guarantee you a pass, but you can be sure of maximising your chances of success.

Planning your study and revision 2

_____

2   Planning your study and revision

Yes, I know, you don't need me lecturing you about all the usual things – make a study timetable, plan your time, find a space for work, be disciplined…. So I won't. If you want to be ill-disciplined about your study, that's fine by me. Just so long as it makes you happy. Happy students learn more.

You don't need a study timetable to be a successful student. In fact, as you probably already know, almost all study timetables are a complete waste of time, as you never stick to them. Thinking that a study timetable will help you to pass the exam is a little bit like thinking you'll get fit by joining a gym, isn't it?

SPENDING HOURS PRODUCING A DETAILED TIMETABLE….

... IS A COMPLETE WASTE OF TIME.

Spending three hours producing a detailed study timetable is a complete waste of three hours. Actually, it's what the psychologists call 'displacement activity' – something you do to avoid doing something else. I don't know anyone who has ever prepared a detailed study timetable and then stuck to it. How can you plan your life in detail for three months or so? I can't even plan my life in detail for the next 24 hours! There's always something that 'just turns up'.

Having a detailed plan and regular routine also makes study feel like 'work' (with all the bad things that are associated with it) rather than 'play' (with all the good things). Any activity is more enjoyable if you allow it to be spontaneous, isn't it?

Your study time is valuable, so spend it studying. Just make up your mind that you'll spend any spare time you have, between now and your exams, studying. Then do it. It'll help if you get a good 'team' around you, to help when your motivation level is low. I don't mean people to nag you, but people to remind you of your priorities and to make your life bearable. For example, it's a lot nicer (and less disruptive to your work) if someone else makes you a cup of tea or coffee every hour, rather than you having to do it yourself. Remember what I said about displacement activity? Well, frequent tea stops are another example. Pretty soon, you start watching the clock and saying, 'just another five minutes and I can have a cup of tea', and that's not very motivating.

Getting your friends and family to give you support is really important. Anyone who has given up smoking, for example, will tell you how much easier it is if you have a sympathetic partner or best friend. Not necessarily someone to share the experience, though that helps a lot (see 'study buddy', later in this chapter), but people who understand that, for a relatively short time, your priorities are changed.

If you want the best motivation tool I can think of, try failure. I know that most books say that 'nothing motivates like success', but I don't agree. I know quite

FAILURE CAN BE A GREAT MOTIVATION.

a few students who have never failed anything – school exams, driving test, university degree – so success is 'normal' to them. Occasionally, one of them fails a CIMA exam, and it's like the end of the world for them. Remember (or imagine, if it's never happened to you) how it feels to be told that you've failed. Trust me, you really don't want that. I'm not suggesting that you go to the extreme of pinning your 'fail letter' to the wall above your desk (as one of my students once did) but you need to get serious about your study.

Do you need a 'defined workspace' to help you to study? That's what a lot of the books tell you but, once again, creating the 'perfect desk' can be a very time-consuming displacement activity. Yes, you need a space for your regular work, and it needs to feel professional and be tidy. You definitely don't need to redecorate a room in your house and buy new 'home office' furniture (again, as one of my students did).

DO YOUR WORK IN THE PLACE THAT WORKS FOR YOU.

When I was a student I used to do most of my study at work. I don't mean in work time (though I'm sure I did some of that, too) but at my desk. There's nowhere better for making you feel professional and organised. When I was a student I wasn't very disciplined (and, come to think of it, nothing much has changed) so I needed to treat study as a job. It worked for me, but working 'at work' doesn't suit everyone. I was lucky in that I worked for an organisation where I had access to the office at pretty much any time of the day or night, but most of my colleagues went home at 5pm. I also had a nice big desk, a comfortable chair, and a coffee machine in easy reach (there's that displacement activity again).

If you're the sort of person who can be reasonably disciplined about study, and you think that studying in your workplace isn't for you, try to make study fun. Well OK, perhaps 'fun' is too strong a word for it, but at least try to make it bearable. The conventional advice about study is to 'make it like the exam', on the basis that your brain needs to associate a particular environment with the information that it's processing. This is fine, when you get nearer to the day of the exams, but it makes for really boring studying. I'm not suggesting that you try to study with the television blaring away in the background, but being comfortable means different things to different people. Personally, I like a comfortable chair (an office chair, not an armchair) and some music playing. However you choose to organise your workspace, you should make sure that you strike a balance between relaxed and businesslike, and that your study time will be at least bearable.

In a later chapter, I'm going to talk about skills development. One of the things I'll discuss is the idea of 'teaching as learning'. I'm not going to go into this in detail now, but if you're going to do it you'll need a friend. I know we accountants aren't famous for our social skills, but I'm not talking about a real friend. I mean a 'study buddy'. Find someone who is planning to sit the same exam(s) as you, at the same time, and who lives reasonably nearby. Then arrange to get together for a couple of hours every week or so. You can meet at your home, or a local library, or even the pub, but it needs to be somewhere you can talk in relative peace. Apart from the educational benefit of discussing topics, having a study buddy will also give you someone to share your stress with!

STUDYING WITH A FRIEND WILL HELP RELIEVE YOUR STRESS.

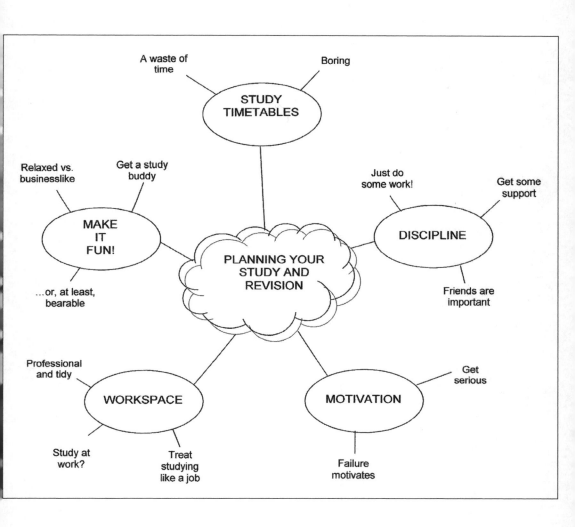

Objective-oriented study **3**

3   Objective-oriented study

What's the point of all this studying? I mean, what's it all for?

Stupid questions? No, not really. They're actually the most important questions to ask yourself, at the beginning of your study time.

Too many students spend far too much time doing things (that they call 'studying') that really don't help their chances of passing the exam. In fact, I reckon that the average diligent student probably wastes at least half of their study time. And, of course, the less 'diligent' you are, the more of your study time you waste.

If you look at Table 1, over the page, you'll see what I think are the 'effectiveness ratings' of the most common study techniques. They're listed in order of popularity, by the way...

Before I get loads of angry letters from lecturers, let me explain something about lectures. Assuming that you have a reasonably good lecturer, lectures can be very valuable but, you need to have realistic expectations. However good your lecturer, they alone can't get you through the exam.

The best thing about a good lecturer is what they can teach you about the exam. You are quite capable of learning material yourself, and you might even have a go at a few questions on your own too, but the big 'value added' from a good lecturer is the insight they can give you into what's expected of you in the exam. That, and the 'pointers' that they give you on how best to focus your efforts.

Revision courses can be a lot more exam-focused than tuition, and they therefore merit a higher effectiveness rating. Some revision courses are just very fast and very focused lecturing, which is good, and can be more effective than longer tuition courses. Other revision courses are based around question practice

Table 1

Effectiveness of study techniques

Study technique	Effectiveness rating
Watching TV	0% (but it feels good)
Reading newspapers and magazines	0–20%
Reading textbooks or study manuals	10–30% (depending on the 'level' of the exam)
Attending lectures (poor lecturer)	20%
Attending lectures (good lecturer)	50%
Attending a revision course	60–80%
Reading past exam papers	20%
Doing 'practice' questions	20%
Reading the syllabus	30%
Reading exam support material	60%
Doing past exam questions	80%

and review, which is about as exam-focused as you can get, but these courses aren't appropriate for you if you've done little or no work beforehand.

Take another look at the effectiveness ratings in Table 1. Have you noticed how I've rated activities that are more exam-focused more highly? This is going to be one of the recurring themes of this book. I call it 'exam-oriented learning'. It's about tailoring all of your preparation to the objective – passing the exam.

In an exam you have to write things, and reading is the opposite of writing. Our brains aren't designed to commit what we read to long-term memory – we train them to read novels, newspapers, and magazines – all things with only short-term interest. If you want to remember something, write it down.

You also need to tailor your learning activities to the level of skill that's going to be tested in the exam, so there's no point in cramming a load of knowledge into your head if the examiner isn't going to ask you what you know. I'll explore this idea in detail in the next chapter but at least you can now see why reading isn't always of much value.

While I'm on the subject of reading, it also matters greatly *what* you read. A lot of lecturers and quite a few 'study guidance' books and articles recommend reading the business press to gather examples for use in the exam. To a great extent this is a waste of time. It might help you to see how the stuff you learn works (or doesn't work) in real life, but there's no need to use real life examples in your answers. The normal rule is: if the examiner wants examples, he'll either ask for them or give you a scenario containing them.

If you're looking for a 'core text' for each exam you're studying for, you need something that was written specifically for the CIMA exams. CIMA's own Learning Systems[1] are, of course, pretty much the most exam-oriented texts you can buy, being written by the examiners. These not only take you through all the syllabus content, but also explain how the material is likely to be examined. There are also plenty of past exam questions, so you can see the sort of thing you might have to do in the exam, and practise a few questions. You need to be very careful with textbooks that were written for some purpose other than helping you to pass your CIMA exams. While many textbooks contain useful background reading and can aid your understanding of core concepts, you still need to do more…

Reading any study material is just the first step towards developing the skills you'll need to pass the exam. There are other things that you can read that will help you to focus your studies on the exam.

---

[1] Learning systems for each of the CIMA exams are available from CIMA publishing at www.cimapublishing.com or by telephone on +44 (0) 1865 474010

If you take another look at Table 1, you'll see that I rate 'reading the syllabus' quite highly. I'm constantly amazed at how few CIMA students bother to do this. When you finish this chapter, get a copy of the syllabus for one of the exams you're about to sit, and take a look at it. Before you do, however, take a look at an article I wrote for CIMA about verbs. There's a copy in Appendix A, and it'll help you to see how important it is to understand the learning outcomes. The syllabus is one of the 'rules of the game' for these exams, so you should know exactly what's 'in' and 'out' before you start studying.

You also need to read the syllabus to help you to understand what 'level' of skills you need to develop in relation to each syllabus topic. As the article in Appendix A says, each learning outcome has a verb, each verb is at a particular level in the 'verb hierarchy', and each level represents a group of similar skills. You need to know 'how far to go' in developing your skills, so you're not taken by surprise when the examiner asks you to do something you haven't prepared yourself to do. You also need to know 'where to stop', as there's no point developing skills that you won't need in the exam.

The balance between how much knowledge you need, and how many 'higher skills' you need to develop depends, to a great extent, on the level of exam you're going to sit. Figure 1 gives a rough illustration of how the marks are allocated to different skills at each level of exam. In the next chapter we'll look at how you can develop those application and analysis skills.

Once you've read the syllabus, and before you even open the Learning System, take a look at a couple of past exam papers. OK, they won't make a lot of sense to you at this early stage, but look at the format of the paper and the style of the questions. What styles of questions are there in each section of the exam paper (objective testing, essays...)? What's the split between compulsory and optional questions? Is the examiner asking what you know? Or for calculations? Or for application to scenarios? All of these things should guide your preparation for the exam.

Even more valuable than past exam papers are the 'post-exam guides' (PEGs)[2] produced by the examiners after each exam. These give a question-by-question

---

[2] You will find the PEGs on the CIMA website at www.cimaglobal.com. Select 'studying' from the top menu, then 'study support' from the left. One of the options should now be 'study resources'. Select this, then the exam you are interested in. The PEGs will be listed. If this doesn't work, or CIMA change their website, just search for 'post exam guide' on the CIMA website

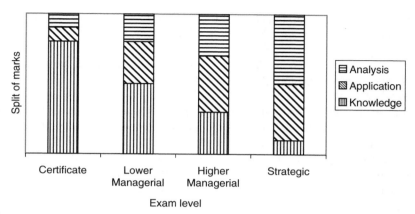

Figure 1
Mark allocation by level of exam

analysis of what the examiner expected students to do, and what they actually did. There's an excerpt from a PEG in Appendix B, and you should look at it now.

You can learn a huge amount about the examiners' expectations by reading their comments in the PEG. You can also see how the marks were awarded, and how much 'leeway' or flexibility there is in the marking scheme. In the PEG in Appendix B, for example, notice how few marks are available for knowledge. This ties in with the skills level analysis in Figure 1. Notice, also, how the marks available for each requirement often add up to more than the total. This shows that there is flexibility in the marking guide, which is typical at the strategic level.

It's really important that you make full use of all the resources that are available. If you look on the CIMA website, you'll find articles and support guides for each exam. The support guides are written to address specific issues, so they're obviously important. The examiners write many of the articles, so it would be stupid not to read them (see chapter 5). You should particularly read any new articles written by the examiner for one of the exams you're about to sit. Such articles may point directly to a question that's coming up on the next exam, so they should form part of your revision materials.

Just before I leave the topic of reading, a word of caution to those of you who are re-sitting a 'wordy' exam (such as Integrated Management, or one of the Strategy papers). I quite often meet students who have sat such an exam three or more times, and each time they sit the exam they get a *lower* mark than they did the previous time! This is despite doing lots of work.

Such students are often surprised that my advice to them is 'stop working'. Now, that sounds ridiculous, but it's not. Let me explain...

If you fail an exam, it's a natural reaction to work harder for your next attempt. Unfortunately, you are likely to do the wrong type of work, and concentrate on improving your knowledge to the point that you 'know everything'. I've met quite a few students, on revision courses, in exactly this position – they can quote the textbook word-for-word. In itself, that's not entirely a bad thing, and it certainly makes my life as a tutor a whole lot easier, but it's what it leads to that causes problems.

A student who has just spent four months learning the entire content of a text-book has only one objective in the exam – to prove how much they know. The reason such students find that their marks decrease is that they forget to just answer the questions, and use the exam as an excuse to rewrite the textbook. This, of course, earns you very few marks.

When I advise resit students to 'stop working', I mean that they should stop cramming loads of knowledge into their heads. Instead, I take them back to basics, and get them to re-read the syllabus and a couple of post-exam guides. I then get them to answer a past exam question, and show them just how easy it would have been to get great marks if only they'd stopped worrying about get-ting loads of theory into their answer and just stuck to answering the question.

That leads me on to my last point in this chapter – doing past exam questions. Once you've understood the syllabus, looked at the exam, read the support materials and got some knowledge, there's only really one thing that adds value. You've just got to do loads of exam-standard questions under exam con-ditions. I know that, for most of you, this is the worst news I could give you, but it's really the only way to improve your chances of passing. Think about it – would you try to pass your driving test without ever having driven a car?

So, to conclude, studying is about working 'smarter', not harder, and focusing your efforts on those study methods that are most likely to lead you to passing your exams.

DON'T WORK HARD....

....WORK SMART.

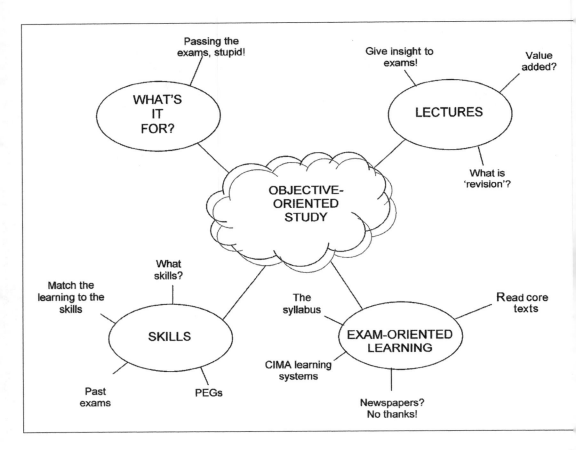

Developing your skills 4

4   Developing your skills

First of all, you need to work out exactly what skills you need...

If you understood the stuff about verbs in the article I referred you to in the previous chapter (Appendix A), you'll remember that the key to defining skills is the learning outcomes in the syllabus. The five different verb levels are shown in Table 2, together with my interpretation of the general type of skills you need to develop at each level. Your learning needs to be progressive, as you can't just 'jump right in' at, for example, level 4. You'll need to start with the knowledge, then move on to the understanding, then the application and so on. This isn't actually as daunting as it sounds, though, because a lot of topics in the higher level exams are repeats of topics you've studied before, but with a higher level of verb.

The key to adequate preparation is to choose a study method that is appropriate to the level of skills that you're trying to develop. Table 3 summarises the applicability of some of the more popular study methods to each of the verb levels. This underlines the limitations of 'reading' as a study method – it really is something to get through as quickly as possible, so you can move on to more productive things. You'll notice that Table 3 doesn't have 'tuition' as one of the study methods listed. This is because your tutors should be getting you to use a range of different study methods (from Table 3) in class.

Let me quickly summarise what these study methods are, and how they can be used.

- Reading: This is just what it says – sitting with a textbook or study manual, reading the words on the page. It's OK for getting the basic knowledge into your head, but that's all. When you read a lot of text it tends to run together, so you start missing bits out. You also won't remember most of what

Table 2

Verbs

	Verb level	Interpretation
1	Knowledge	You just have to know it – knowledge of facts, theories, techniques
2	Comprehension	You have to understand it – hypothetical strengths and weaknesses, background, history, relationships between different topics
3	Application	You have to be able to do it – application of your knowledge to a range of different contexts
4	Analysis	You have to be able to look at practical situations and identify problems. You also have to be able to take a proposed solution, apply it, then discuss the issues arising from that application
5	Evaluation	You have to be able to identify possible solutions, discuss their strengths and weaknesses, then recommend and justify what you believe to be the most appropriate

Table 3

Verbs and study methods

Verb level		Study method								
		Reading	Summarising	Article study	Simulation	Discussions	Role-playing	Case studies	Presentations	Teaching
1	Knowledge	☑	☑	☑	☑	☑	☑	☑	☑	☑
2	Comprehension	☐	☑	☑	☑	☑	☑	☑	☑	☑
3	Application	☐	☐	☑	☑	☑	☑	☑	☑	☑
4	Analysis	☐	☐	☐	☐	☑	☑	☑	☑	☑
5	Evaluation	☐	☐	☐	☐	☐	☑	☑	☑	☑

you read. 'Highlighting' (with a highlighter pen, or underlining) doesn't really have any advantages, other than marginally increasing recall.

- Summarising: This is really just effective reading. If you want to make something memorable, turn your study from a passive activity (reading) to an active activity (writing). The idea is that, in order to get from your eyes (input) to your hand (output) the information has to go through your brain (processing). Thus, you remember it more effectively. Don't just copy things out longhand, though. Develop a note-taking style that suits your preferred learning style (see later) such as mind-maps, lists or tables.
- Article study: This can be a very effective way to develop application skills. Find an article, from the business press, that describes or discusses a real organisation (or industry) using the technique/approach/model/theory that you are studying. The problem is finding a good, relevant article about a piece of theory that you (by definition) don't know much about. This is where a good tutor can help – by finding useful articles to assist your study.
- Simulation: For developing application skills, I can't think of any better way than this. Once you've learned the basics of a technique or theory, invent 'contexts' in which it might be applied. Think of three or four different types and sizes of organisation, then think what the issues and problems might be in applying the theory to each of those contexts. You can do this over and over again, and don't throw your 'contexts' away – they'll come in handy for the next theory or model, and the next.... To help you, I've included some sample contexts in Appendix C.
- Discussions: You can do this in class, or with your study buddy, but it's not easy to do if you study alone! Talk about the topic you're studying. Express your concerns. If anyone says 'I don't know', find out! There's a lot of potential synergy in study groups – you'll often find that what one person finds difficult, another finds easy.
- Role-playing: This one's really difficult to do on your own! It also needs some planning and co-ordination. Write a short scenario that's relevant to the area you're studying, including a brief 'biography' of each of the 'players' (you'll need the same number of players as members of the study group, minus one for a moderator). Then get the players to 'act out' their roles, raising and dealing with issues that might arise in real life.
- Case studies: These are often used in the higher level CIMA exams, as well as being the assessment method used in the TOPCIMA exam. You can use old exam question scenarios for case study materials, or get some from the many websites that have them for download. You can even use newspaper and magazine articles, but these are often too 'light' in terms of facts relevant to the CIMA syllabus. Once you've found your scenario, just answer the following questions: What are the major issues in this situation? How can

what I've learnt help me to diagnose the problems and identify potential solutions? What are the alternative solutions? Which would I recommend, and why?

- Presentations: I often use this technique in class – getting one (or a few) of my students to prepare and deliver a short presentation to the group – and I always get the same comment. 'Why do I have to do this, when I'm not allowed to give a presentation in the exam?' The answer? It's a great way to develop your confidence, and it gives a clear objective to your study. It's also very useful knowing that your friends are going to ask you all sorts of awkward questions at the end of your presentation. You'll tend to over-prepare, which is a good thing.
- Lecturing: Trainee doctors have a saying – 'watch one, do one, teach one'. It was only when I became a lecturer that I realised just how little I knew. Knowing that you're going to have to teach others makes you very serious about your learning, and the actual process of teaching is a great way to learn. I'm not suggesting that you should go out and get a job as a freelance CIMA lecturer, though there are colleges out there that really want Strategic Level students to teach their Managerial Level classes. No, I'm suggesting that you have short 'teach-ins', where one of you teaches the other a new topic. You can do this in a study group, or with your study buddy but, once again, it's really difficult to do if you're studying on your own.

The idea of 'watch one, do one, teach one' is similar to the 'learning cycle'. Developing skills is a process, with a beginning and end. Of course, there can be iteration (repeated processes) but it's reasonable to look at learning like this. I like simple models, such as 'study, review, practise, reflect'. If you break your work down into 'bite-sized chunks', then follow the learning cycle for each 'chunk', your study will be more effective. The stages are as follows:

1. Study: Determine the topic scope and skill level for the 'chunk' that you're going to study next. Pick an appropriate learning technique. Find a friend, if required. Study the topic.
2. Review: Make some brief notes on what you've learnt. These will come in handy when you're revising the topic, closer to the date of the real exam.
3. Practise: Have a go at a couple of past exam questions on the topic. Remember – this is the most 'exam-oriented' study you can do. Don't just read the questions and say 'I can do that'! Have a go, and review your answer against the post-exam guide (Questions and answers from CIMA publishing).
4. Reflect: See what lessons you can learn from the first three steps of the learning cycle. Did the process highlight any weaknesses in your skills? Go and fix the problem(s) now, by going through the learning cycle again (iteration).

You'll notice that most of the learning methods in Table 3 are very 'active'. I'm a big fan of what I call 'activity-based learning', as I think it makes learning not just more effective but also more bearable. I'm not going to say it's always 'enjoyable', but if we can make it relatively painless, the time will pass much more quickly.

TRY TO MAKE YOUR LEARNING ACTIVE RATHER THAN PASSIVE.

Table 3 is only a selection of study methods. The one(s) you prefer will depend, to a great extent, on your preferred 'learning style'. This is the way your brain prefers to work, and is something that you develop in adolescence. The major learning styles are shown in Table 4, together with some of the more practical ways you can build relevant activities into your learning.

So, if you were sitting there thinking 'I like the idea of doing case studies, but presentations scare me' it might just be because you're not an auditory learner. If you want to see which style(s) you favour, have a go at the diagnostic test in Table 5. It's only a quick test, of course, so it's not foolproof. Also, don't be surprised if you're classified as two styles, or even all three. It's more about identifying the sorts of learning tools to avoid, than which to use exclusively.

Regardless of your preferred learning style, most of you will prefer *not* to learn lists. This is because of the way the brain prefers to work. Lists are a 'left brain' technique and, though we train our brains to use such techniques, they (our brains)

Table 4

Learning styles and study tools

Style	Nature	Study tool(s)
Visual	Need to see the teacher's body language and facial expression to fully understand the content of a lesson. Tend to prefer sitting at the front of the classroom to avoid visual obstructions (e.g. people's heads). May think in pictures.	Diagrams, illustrated textbooks, overhead transparencies, videos, flipcharts and hand-outs.
Auditory	Interpret the underlying meanings of speech through listening to tone of voice, pitch, speed and other nuances. Written information may have little meaning until it is heard.	Verbal lectures, discussions, talking things through and listening to what others have to say. These learners often benefit from reading text aloud and using a tape recorder.
Kinesthetic/ Tactile	May find it hard to sit still for long periods and may become distracted by their need for activity and exploration.	Learn best through a hands-on approach, actively exploring the physical world around them. Enjoy role-playing and games.

remain dominated by their right side. That's the part of the brain that responds to music, pattern, colour, and movement.

Rather than using lists, for your note-taking and revision, try to use 'mind-maps'. These were first developed in the 1970s by Tony Buzan, specifically as a way for students to make notes. All you do is put the 'core theme' in a box or 'bubble' in the middle of the page, then create your notes in a series of further bubbles around the first. Yes, that's right, just like the 'summary' diagrams at the end of each chapter of this book!

There aren't many rules for mind mapping. The whole point is that it should work for you. Use short words and phrases, or even little cartoons and diagrams. Use colour, and link related topics or points. That's it really. Mind maps are effective because they're very easy to recall, and because they work in the same way as the brain (as a relational database, if you're interested). I tend to do all my teaching (and particularly my 'revision' courses) by creating a series

Table 5

Determining your learning style (*Adapted from Colin Rose (1987). Accelerated Learning*)

When you..	Visual	Auditory	Kinesthetic/Tactile
Spell	Do you try to see the word? 3	Do you sound out the word or use a phonetic approach? 1	Do you write the word down to find if it feels right? 2
Talk	Do you talk sparingly and dislike listening for too long? Do you favour words such as *see, picture,* and *imagine*? 3	Do you enjoy listening but are impatient to talk? Do you use words such as *hear, tune,* and *think*? 2	Do you gesture and use expressive movements? Do you use words such as *feel, touch,* and *hold*? 1
Concentrate	Do you become distracted by untidiness or movement? 2	Do you become distracted by sounds or noises? 3	Do you become distracted by activity around you? 1
Meet someone again	Do you forget names but remember faces or remember where you met? 2	Do you forget faces but remember names or remember what you talked about? 3	Do you remember best what you did together? 1
Contact people on business	Do you prefer direct, face-to-face, personal meetings? 1	Do you prefer the telephone? 3	Do you talk with them while walking or participating in an activity? 2
Read	Do you like descriptive scenes or pause to imagine the action? 2	Do you enjoy dialogue and conversation or hear the characters talk? 3	Do you prefer action stories or are not a keen reader? 1
Do something new at work	Do you like to see demonstrations, diagrams, slides, or posters? 1	Do you prefer verbal instructions or talking about it with someone else? 3	Do you prefer to jump right in and try it? 2
Put something together	Do you look at the directions and the picture? 1	Do you ask someone to 'talk me through it'? 3	Do you ignore the directions and figure it out as you go along? 2
Need help with a computer application	Do you seek out pictures or diagrams? 3	Do you call the help desk, ask a neighbour, or growl at the computer? 2	Do you keep trying to do it or try it on another computer? 1
	16	23	15

of colour mind maps. I also suggest that students use them for answer planning, though that's discussed in detail in a later chapter. For now, take a look at Appendix D where I've included an example of a mind map for an exam topic.

So, to conclude, you need to find a way (or ways) of studying that suit both your preferred learning style and the type of skill you're trying to develop. Change the way you make notes, to make them more memorable, and try to make your learning active rather than passive.

LOSE THE LIST, GET YOUR HEAD ROUND 'MIND-MAPS'.

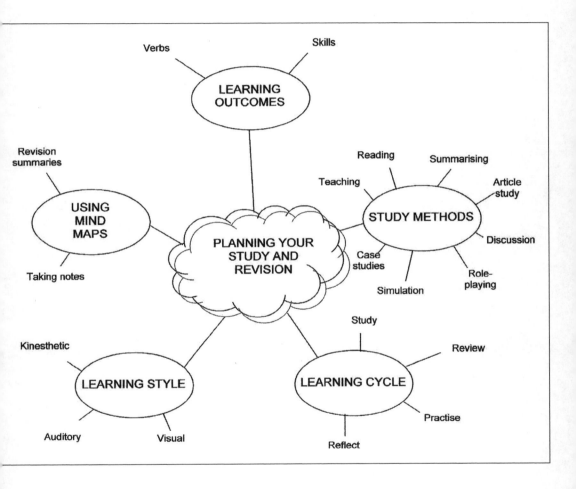

Know your examiner(s) 5

5 Know your examiner(s)

I think that you really need to know about your examiners' academic and business, likes and dislikes and their 'favourite things'. Why? Because examiners

KNOW YOUR EXAMINERS.

are more likely to examine the things they teach, research or consult on than any others. It may be that more scenarios on the exam are based in an industry that the examiner used to work in, or that certain topics get over-examined because the examiner does research on those areas.

Of course, there are ways to work out how your examiner thinks. You could (and should) download and read all of the past exams and post-exam guides (PEGs) from the CIMA website. I mentioned PEGs a couple of chapters ago, and even put an example in Appendix B. If you don't have the PEGs for your next set of CIMA exams yet, go and get them now.

Putting together a series of four or five past exams, with their PEGs, you'll be able to see any patterns in the questions. Look out for styles, recurring issues, patterns (such as major topics alternating or 'cycling') or common contexts. This is just one more way to get an 'edge' in your next exams.

While you've got a series of past exams and PEGs in front of you, there's something else you can do. The examiners have to examine their whole syllabus, and this means setting a series of exams that eventually contain questions about every learning outcome. Get on your PC (or get a piece of paper) and set up a table like the one shown in Table 6. The reason I suggest using your PC is that you can update the table after each set of exams, if necessary.

I've just done the first few lines for Paper P5 (Integrated Management) in Table 6. I've also 'invented' the content, so those of you sitting for the P5 exam will have to redo the analysis for yourselves. The learning outcomes are straight from the syllabus, and you might be able to 'cut and paste' them from the downloadable document of the CIMA website. To find out which learning outcome each question relates to, you'll have to read the PEG and the exam paper. Sometimes the PEG will say which learning outcome is being examined, other times you'll have to work it out for yourself.

What's the point? Take another look at Table 6. Assuming you're planning to sit for the November 2007 P5 exam, and assuming my analysis to be accurate, you might make a number of assumptions about the pattern of questions in the paper:

- It looks like learning outcome A(i) is normally examined in May, but not November.
- Learning outcome A(ii) has been examined rather a lot recently, so maybe it's less likely to be examined in November.
- It's a long time (five exams) since learning outcome A(iii) was examined, so maybe that makes it more likely to be examined next time.

Table 6

Learning outcomes control sheet

Learning outcome (Paper P5)	M05	N05	M06	N06	M07
A(i) – explain the process of strategy formulation	1.2		4c		2c
A(ii) – evaluate different organisation structures		1.8		1.5	2b
A(iii) – discuss concepts in contemporary	3a				
And so on...					

Of course, you've got to be very careful with this kind of analysis. First, the trend is often not long enough for true patterns to emerge. Second, examiners spot such trends too, and can choose to deliberately 'break' them. And, finally, it's far too risky to ignore a topic just because you think it won't be examined. I use analyses like these for 'fine tuning' my students' last-minute revision. I make sure that they've covered the whole syllabus, but then get them to spend just a little extra time on the 'hot' topics that seem more likely to be examined this time.

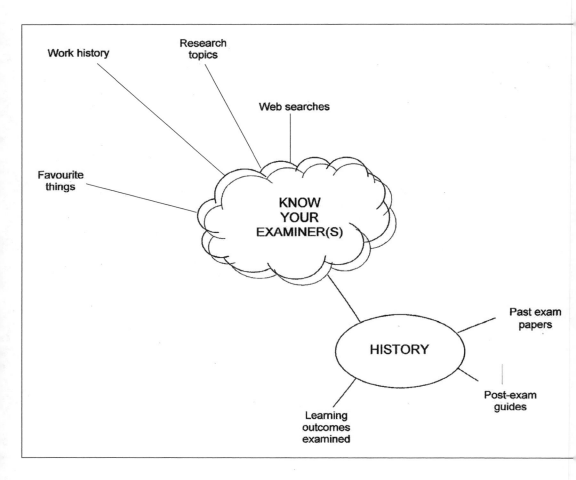

Cool those nerves 6

6 Cool those nerves

Exam stress is a problem for everyone. I've never met a student who didn't get stressed at some point during the exam process. I reckon that, for the 'average' student (whatever one of those is) exam stress probably costs them ten marks. That's ten marks that they deserved to get, but lost out on because the stress of the exam caused them to make a stupid mistake like choosing the wrong optional question, or mis-reading a question requirement.

STRESS....

If you know that stress is a significant issue for you, it might cost you far more than ten marks. In extreme cases, I know of students who couldn't even go into the exam room, or had to leave after ten minutes, because the stress was so bad. If you're sitting there reading this and getting tense, you might have a problem.

What can you really do to limit the level of stress? I say 'limit', because we actually don't want to get rid of all the stress. A little bit of stress is a good thing, because it gets the adrenalin flowing and sharpens our senses. No, we want to get rid of the destructive stress that loses us marks. Try these simple tactics for stress reduction:

- As you get closer to the date of the exam, gradually change your learning environment to be more similar to the exam room. If you prefer sitting in a comfortable chair for your work, replace it with a hard one. Find a small desk or table, and make sure that its surface is clear of any 'junk'. Place your desk against a blank wall so that there are no distractions. Make sure that you gradually 'fade out' any distractions, such as playing music. You might even spend the last few weeks revising in a library, where the atmosphere is more like that of the exam room.
- Rehearse the day of the exam several times, by travelling to the exam centre at the same time of day as you will for the real exam. Make sure that you know the route, and have details of parking or public transport. Have a contingency plan, just in case your chosen form of transport is unavailable. Arrange for a friend to be available to give you a lift, in case of emergencies. If it's your first time at this exam centre, ask if you can have a look inside the exam room.
- Find somewhere reasonably quiet that you can sit, while you're waiting for the exam, close to the exam centre but away from other students. It might be a coffee shop, a library, or even a park. Being surrounded by stressed people is bound to increase your stress level. Too much coffee is bad for stress, by the way, so avoid it on the day of the exam. Drink water, but not too much or you'll be spending more time out of the exam than in it!
- Make sure that you have a list of things to do on the day before (and morning of) the exam. If you are kept busy, you won't have time to get stressed.
- Practise relaxation techniques, such as deep breathing or visualising a 'happy place'. There are a number of websites full of very useful advice. Find two or three methods that suit you, and start using them a few weeks before the exam. Make sure that you practise these techniques at least three times a day, every day.

To conclude, you need to work out how to manage your stress levels, as a little bit of stress is good but a lot is definitely bad.

... AND HOW TO USE IT.

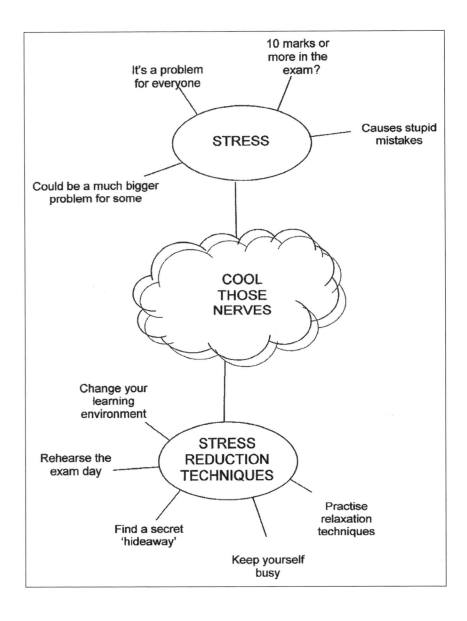

What examiners and markers want 7

7 What examiners and markers want

Who are the examiners, what do they do, and why on earth do they want to do what they do? These are perfectly valid questions, though the answers might surprise you.

Most of the examiners are academics. They work in universities and business schools, and are generally senior lecturers in business-related areas. This means that the examiners have a good knowledge of the syllabus content, or at least major parts of it, but may never have 'done' what they teach. This might lead to a more 'academic' (i.e. 'by the book') approach in the exam, which should-n't cause the majority of students a problem, because they've learnt it from books anyway. It can, however, be a different approach for students who *have* actually 'done' it.

The examiners aren't responsible for writing the syllabus, so they aren't really in control of what they examine. Sure, they can make suggestions for syllabus changes, but it might take a while for the changes to be made. Their job is to examine the learning outcomes in their syllabus, in such a way that they allow markers to discriminate between acceptable and unacceptable performance levels.

There are other things that the examiners are *not* responsible for, too. They don't decide on the structure of their exam paper, for example. As an examiner, I have no control over whether my exam has objective test questions and, if so, how many. Nor can I decide how much of my exam is compulsory, or how much choice is given in the optional section(s). All that is decided by CIMA.

The examiners are controlled to ensure that their exams are a fair and reason-able test. The papers go through a very complicated and time-consuming process to ensure that they're technically correct and free from errors. The impact that the examiner has is in terms of the 'feel' of the exam (how long the sce-narios are, and what type of organisations are described), and which learning outcomes are examined at each specific sitting, and at what 'level' (application, analysis, etc.).

So, why do the examiners do the job? Well, it's just that – a job. They just want to set fair but challenging exams. They really want you to pass their exams, but only if you're good enough. CIMA decides what is meant by 'good enough' in terms of the different skills required to be a management accountant, and the examiners set exams to test those skills.

Provided your answers are either reasonably good or really bad, the examiners are never going to see them. That's because there are so many candidates that each examiner has a team of markers to decide whether each candidate passes or fails. The examiners themselves generally only see the 'marginal' attempts.

The markers are a diverse group of individuals – some of them are tutors, others are CIMA members, some of them teach, others don't. What you need to remember is that, like the examiners, the markers are there to do a job. They don't know who you are, as the exam scripts don't identify you, it is an anony-mous process. They have no way of knowing whether this is your first attempt at the exam, or the latest in a long series. They're just interested in deciding whether you have displayed the right skills to pass the exam. If you're good enough, they're happy for you to pass.

All the marker looks for is whether you earn 50 or more marks. In fact, they're much happier if you do pass. The marks relate to the skills that you demonstrate in your answers, and 50 is the point at which the examiner has decided that you're good enough. Because the marker has to be able to read and understand your answers, and decide whether you're displaying the right skills, the way you communicate with the marker is really important (as we'll see in Chapter 11).

It's important for you to stop now, for a moment, to think about what you've just learned. The examiners and markers would actually prefer it if you passed! The easier your answers are to mark, the more likely you are to pass.

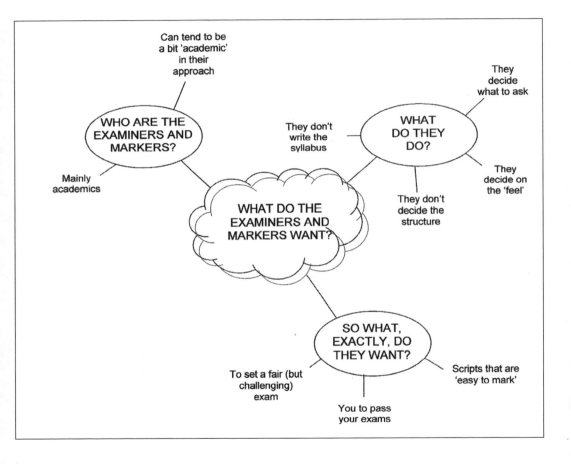

The formula 8

8   The formula

Students always ask me, 'is there a secret to success in the CIMA exams'? Well, obviously there is, so I tell them what it is. If you want to significantly improve your chances of passing the CIMA exams, there are three simple steps to success – read the question, understand the question, answer the question. That's it.

What do you mean, 'that's a bit obvious'? Let me explain...

The vast majority of 'mistakes' made by candidates in their CIMA exams are nothing to do with imperfect or absent knowledge. They're about *not* answering the question the examiner asked. Most commonly, students will do the following:

- Mis-read the question, and answer the one they 'thought' was there, rather than the one that was really there.
- Identify a key word or phrase in the question, and write 'all they know' about that topic.
- Answer a version of the question asked, but fail to address the verb in the question.
- Answer the first 'task' in a question requirement, but ignore any subsequent task(s).

Let's have a look at each of these in more detail, starting with mis-reading the question.

One of the biggest problems with these exams is the stress level they generate. While I dealt with ways to reduce stress in a previous chapter, there's still going to be a 'residual' degree of stress that makes you do stupid things. For example, one of the effects of stress is an increase in adrenalin. This is normally a good thing, as it allows you to think and act more quickly, but adrenalin does have some nasty side effects. One of these is that you can tend to lack concentration.

One of the most important things you have to do is read the questions really, *really* carefully. Then read them again. And again. After all, if you don't know what the question is, how can you answer it? It's really important that you answer precisely the question that's there, as the marking guide (that the examiner gives to the markers) assumes that you'll do this. There's always some leeway in the marking guide, particularly in 'wordy' papers, but there is a basic assumption that you'll do pretty much what the examiner asked you to do.

...SPEND MORE TIME ON THE QUESTION.

Writing 'everything I know' about the topic of a question, or something related to it, is a common student error. At the 'lower' levels of the CIMA exams, like the early Managerial level papers, you might be able to get away with this approach, as the verbs used in the questions are more likely to ask for your knowledge. At the higher levels of Managerial Level, and particularly at the Strategic Level, giving the marker a 'brain dump' of everything you've learned is unlikely to earn you many (if any) marks. That's because the verb level (see Appendix A) used in these exams is much more likely to be application or evaluation, rather than knowledge.

To some extent I can understand why students write this kind of answer, as I'm sure I did when I was a student. It's the temptation to prove just how much work you've done, and how much you've learned. The irony is that, although exam questions are always *related* to the material in the learning systems (or textbooks), they seldom ask for *exactly* that material. The examiners really want to see whether you understand it, not how 'photographic' your memory is.

In an earlier chapter I talked about how to increase the effectiveness of your learning by doing stuff that's more directly related to the exams. Maybe the 'brain dump' answer is a symptom of a student who's memorised the textbook rather than practising questions?

Answering the 'wrong' verb is a common problem, and often a symptom of the candidate not understanding the meaning of the verb, or not having the skills required to address the verb in the question. It's very common for examiners, particularly at the 'higher' levels, to ask students to 'advise' or 'evaluate', only to get a load of answers that only 'explain' or 'discuss'. If you're still not sure what I mean, have another read of the article in Appendix A.

Finally, in this section about the different ways to mis-answer the questions, there are those questions where the examiner asks you to do more than one thing. I don't mean the common 'part (a), part (b), etc.' questions. Having more than one 'requirement' in a question is almost normal on many of the higher level papers. I mean those questions where the examiner asks you to do more than one thing *within* a requirement. Let me give you an example...

(a) *Briefly explain what is meant by a 'mission statement', and recommend a suitable*
　　 mission statement for X plc.　　　　　　　　　　　　　　　　*(10 marks)*

In this question, there are clearly two 'tasks' (specific things to do) – first, to explain what is meant by a 'mission statement' and, second, to recommend a suitable mission statement for X plc. At first glance, you could be forgiven for assuming that each task is likely to be worth five marks, as there are ten available for the whole requirement. However, look at the difference in the verbs used in each task.

The first task (the 'explain') is at a very low verb level, whereas the second (the 'recommend') is at the highest verb level. The first task also has a 'briefly' as a signal not to spend too much time on this part of the requirement. So, it's quite likely that there are 2–4 marks for the first task, and 6–8 for the second. So, even if you make a really good job of answering the first task, you can't get more than half marks without a reasonable attempt at the second.

That said, why would any of you *deliberately* not answer the second task? Well, I think it's most likely to be a combination of carelessness and poor planning. If you read the requirement, you immediately think 'right, I need to explain mission statements', and you do just that. Then you think you've finished the requirement and you move on to part (b), or the next question. Planning your answer carefully can avoid this happening, as we'll see in the next chapter.

Just before we move on to answer planning, a word about objective testing (OT) questions. While there's very little 'exam technique' involved in objective testing, some of the messages of this book do apply. Believe it or not, it's still amazingly common for candidates to *not* answer OT questions, you must, as there's no penalty for getting them wrong. Always, *always* have a guess at OT questions, even if you don't have a clue what they're about. Having said that, it's often possible to rule out one of the answers as being completely unreasonable, so just guessing from the remaining three will get you a third of the marks (on a purely random basis).

Come to think of it, 'have a go' is quite a good bit of advice for any exam question. There are very few guarantees in exams, but one of them is – if you write nothing, you'll get no marks! I often see student answers with gaps, where the students have convinced themselves that they don't know anything, or haven't got a clue what the question means. It's always worth taking a guess, as there are no 'negative' (or penalty) marks in these exams.

So, to summarise, the key to avoiding the most common mistakes in these exams is to slow down a bit. You need to spend a bit more time on the questions, and a bit less time on the answers. Don't be in too much of a hurry to answer, make sure that you know exactly what the question is before you do, and always 'have a go'.

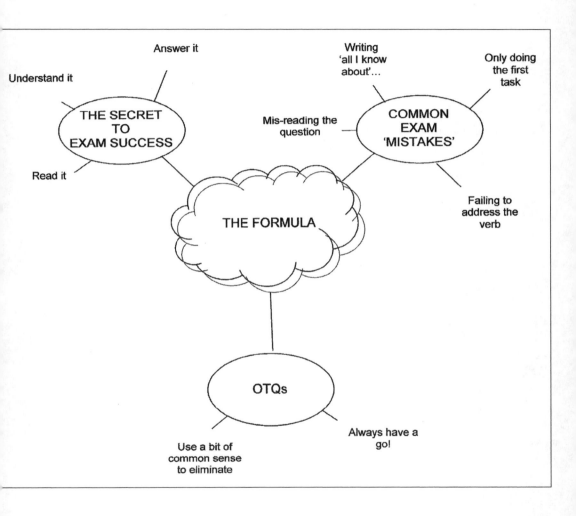

Answer planning 9

9   Answer planning

In the previous chapter, I mentioned spending a bit more time on the questions in order to reduce the risk of not answering them. One of the best ways of doing this is to do a good, structured answer plan. So, I guess the logical way to start a chapter on answer planning is to explain what I mean (and *don't* mean) by an answer plan.

What I certainly *don't* mean is a list of ideas or brief bullet points. Many of my students tell me that they think answer plans are a waste of time because 'you just end up doing everything twice'. Well, if you plan badly, that may well be the case. What you need is a method of planning that isn't just about making brief notes. Let's start from the basics...

Any exam question has three key elements:
1. A topic (what the question is about, or the piece of knowledge that's being tested),
2. a verb (to tell you what approach to take when answering the question), and
3. a mark allocation (that gives you an indication of how many points to cover in your answer, and how long to spend answering).

Some questions, those with a scenario, also have useful facts that might help you to produce a good answer. Finally, of course, you also need your knowledge to help you to 'add value' to your answer. A good answer plan, therefore, is one that allows you to combine these four (or five, if there's a scenario) elements to produce a good answer that earns most of the available marks.

SPEND MORE TIME PLANNING YOUR ANSWER

To me, the point of answer planning is to improve the quality of your answer (and therefore earn more marks) while reducing the risk of making a mistake and answering a question that isn't actually there. Let me demonstrate, step by step, how I would develop an answer plan for a real CIMA past-exam question. The question I'll use is from the November 2005 Paper P6 exam, and it's reproduced in full in Appendix E. Read through it now.

The approach to answer planning that I favour, and that I teach my students, uses a very structured kind of mind map. Each requirement of the question, and each task within each requirement, gets its own 'branch' of the mind map, into which I put a summary of the question requirement or task. Each summary clearly shows the topic, verb and mark allocation, as shown in Figure 2.

The next step in my planning process would be to decide how many 'points' (or arguments) I need to put into my answer, for each requirement. In the case of this question, the examiner for Paper P6 tends to award an average of 2 marks for each point. I know this because I've studied the Post-Exam Guides (PEGs) for P6[3], and the marking guides show the examiner consistently using the 'rule of 2' in allocating marks to points. Once I've decided how many points to try to find, for each requirement, I add 'arms' to the mind map as shown in Figure 3.

You'll notice, looking at Figure 3, that the arms on each task form different patterns. That's because of the different verbs used. In requirement (a) the verb is 'discuss', so I've taken the 'odd' mark from the 15 and decided to give a

---
[3] We looked at PEGs in the chapter on Exam-oriented study

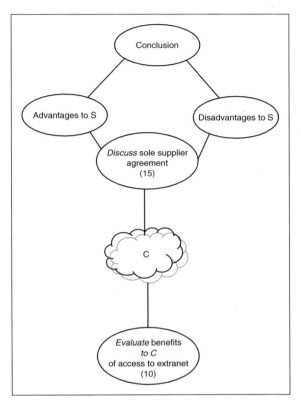

Figure 2
Answer plan step 1

conclusion as to whether, in general terms, the arrangement is advantageous or disadvantageous to S. In requirement (b), the verb is 'evaluate', so I've assumed that the first mark is for stating the benefit, and the second for the 'evaluation' (i.e. saying whether the benefit is substantial or minor).[4]

So far, my answer planning for this question has consisted only of a careful analysis of the question, and some assumptions about mark allocation and the approach required. These are the steps that really make the answer plan a 'damage limitation' tool. If you start your planning by spending a bit more time on analysing the question, you're much less likely to answer a question that isn't there.

---

[4] If you're still unsure about the meanings of the different verbs, re-read the article in Appendix A

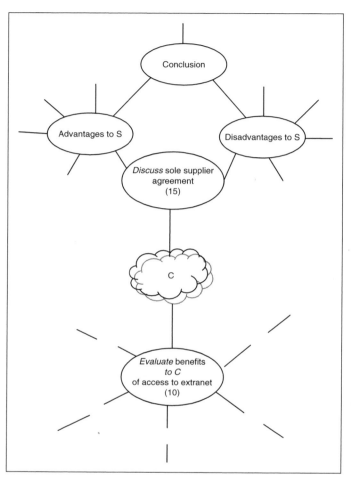

Figure 3
Answer plan step 2

Anyway, having finished analysing the question, I now need to start generating the points to go into my answer. I could, of course, just brainstorm possible advantages, disadvantages and benefits, and write them on the 'arms' of the mind map. However, I'm not going to do that, for two reasons: First, some of the points may not be relevant to S, in this situation, so I'd have to check each point against the scenario. Second, it's quite likely that the examiner will have put some 'clues' into the scenario, to help me find the points that I need. If I look for the clues first, I don't need to think as hard, and I'll know that

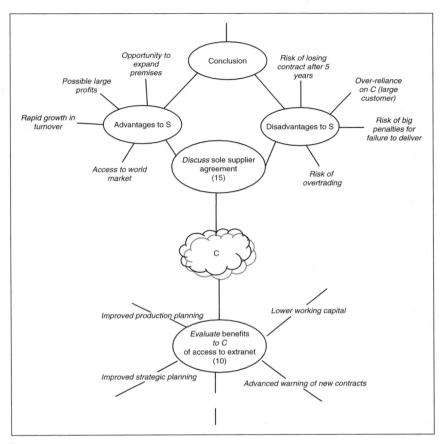

Figure 4
Answer plan step 3

all the points I generate will be relevant to the situation described in the scenario.

Before you look at the mind map for the next stage of the plan, take another look at the scenario for the question (in Appendix E). Even if you haven't been taught anything about the relevant topics, see if you can spot any possible points to go onto the answer plan.

Having done the analysis myself, my plan now looks like Figure 4. You'll notice, from Figure 4, that I've managed to find quite a few clues in the scenario. Interestingly, there are now enough points on my answer plan to pass the question. All I'd have to do is write each point in my answer in such a way as to make it worth 2 marks.[5] Anyway, if I want to try for 'full marks' I'll need to think about what I've been taught, to try to find a few more points. As I've 'invented' these points (rather than basing them on 'clues' in the scenario) I'll have to check that each is valid in the situation described in the scenario.

Having finished generating (and 'testing') points, I need to complete my plan by filling in any gaps. In the case of this question, that means concluding in requirement (a), and adding in the 'evaluation' of each point in requirement (b). Having done this, my completed plan looks like Figure 5.

Now that I'm happy with my plan, I'll need to write out my answer. This is the subject of the next chapter, which is all about 'writing for marks'.

Just before we finish looking at answer planning, we need to think about the different question styles in each of the exams. Firstly, we need to decide whether answer planning works for each of them. Secondly, we need to decide what form an answer plan might take, for each different question style.

There's obviously no benefit in planning your answer to an objective test question. You might as well just do the calculation, or (hopefully) pick the right answer from the list.

In 'short answer' questions, such as those found in papers P1, P4, and P7, you will probably find that a brief plan will help more than you expect. In these questions, particularly the fairly unstructured scenario-based questions found in paper P4, it's very easy to go 'off course' and lose quite a few relatively easy marks. You'll find an example of a short answer section from paper P4 in Appendix F.

The 'calculate and explain' questions, such as those found in papers P1, P2, P7, and P8 need a slightly modified approach. Before doing the answer plan for the 'explain' part of the question, you need to do all of the 'calculate' part. Some or most of the explanation or discussion points will obviously depend on the outcome of the calculations. An example of a plan for this style of question is in Appendix G.

---

[5] See the next chapter for how to make a point worth two marks

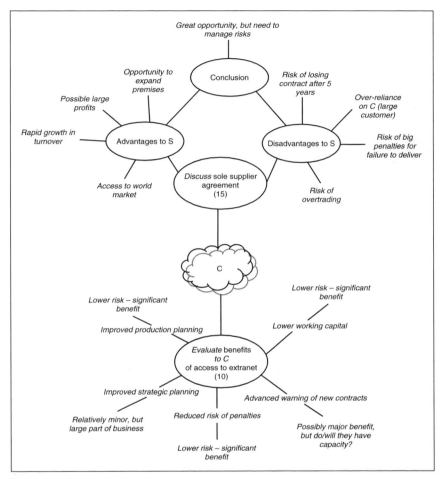

Figure 5
Answer plan step 4

Let me summarise the advice I've given on planning. Answer plans, when done the right way, are a very useful control mechanism. They should significantly reduce the risk of your answer 'going off course'. A good plan should be a vehicle for detailed analysis of the question, and should allow you to assemble the essential components of a really good answer. However, simple 'list of points' answer plans are a waste of time.

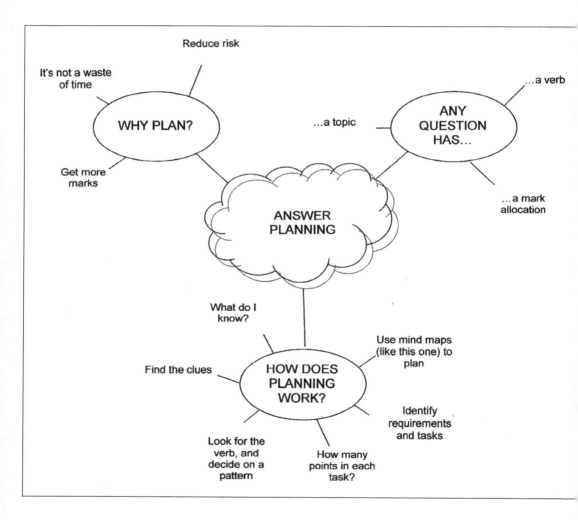

Writing for marks 10

10 Writing for marks

You might think it strange that I've chosen to include a chapter in this book on how to write, but you mustn't underestimate the importance of 'the words on the page'. Very few of us actually write anything any more, so we've forgotten just how to produce good, handwritten, narrative. Maybe, at some point in the future, you'll be allowed to do your CIMA exams by SMS message but, for now, let's remind ourselves how to write...

In order to make your written answers easy to read and understandable, you need to structure your arguments into sentences and paragraphs. Let me start by giving you a quick, but exam-focused, reminder.

The sentence is the basic component of communication. It is a collection of words that, together, achieve a number of objectives:

- It says something. In other words, it contains a 'point' or an 'argument'.
- It makes sense. In other words, when it is read, the message is clear and understandable.
- It gets a mark. In other words, it contains something that 'adds value' to your answer and is thus worthy of some reward from the marker.

One of the biggest problems of these exams is time pressure. I think that one of the best ways to ease that pressure is to write less. However, if you don't write very much, there's a risk that you won't get enough marks to pass. My solution is for you to make sure that every single sentence you write has the potential to earn a mark. In theory, that should mean that you could pass one of your exams with an answer (in total) of only fifty sentences. I wouldn't recommend this strategy, however, as it's very high risk!

A good sentence has certain characteristics that will help it to achieve the objectives outlined above:

- It should be short. Any more than about twenty words and the sentence runs the risk of confusing the reader.
- It shouldn't contain too much punctuation. Sentences are much easier to read (and understand) if they have either no punctuation at all, or just a single comma somewhere in them. Any more complex than that and a typical reader will have to read the sentence two or three times to be sure of understanding it.[6]
- It should make its point clearly and concisely. These exams are not about elegant language and beautiful prose. They're about getting your message across.

Most of the points or arguments that you'll be making in these exams, particularly at the Strategic level, will (or should) be quite complex. Too complex, in fact, for a single sentence. That's where paragraphs come in handy.

A paragraph is a group of related sentences that, together, communicate a point or argument. A good paragraph, therefore, has the following characteristics:

- It consists of a group of two, three, or four sentences.
- Those sentences are all related to each other, and to the point or argument being made.
- Each of the sentences 'builds on' the previous one(s) to develop the point or argument.
- The paragraph deals with the point or argument in its entirety (in other words, a further paragraph is not required).

When I'm writing any business communication, such as this book for example, I try to follow a simple rule for paragraphs. I call it the 'I.C.I.' rule. I try to make my three sentences 'Introduce' the point, 'Clarify' the point and, if necessary, 'Illustrate' the point.

Look at it another way: Let your first sentence make the point or argument in a concise manner. Read that sentence, and then write another sentence that explains (or 'clarifies') why the first sentence is true. Then read the two sentences again and, if they're still not perfectly clear, write a third sentence with an example or practical reference (illustration) that helps to prove the point.

I appreciate that this idea is a bit complicated, so you might want to re-read the previous three paragraphs. Think about the ideas – they don't always work, but they can completely change the way you write. You also need to practise. A lot!

I've included, in Appendix H, an examiner's suggested answer to one of the questions we produced an answer plan for in the previous chapter. Take a look at it and see if the examiner has followed some or most of the 'rules' for sentences and paragraphs.

While we're on the subject of writing, lots of students ask me about the importance of spelling and punctuation. I always tell them the same thing. 'If the markers can't read it, they can't mark it'! These exams are not a test of your written English skills, so any marker will ignore weaknesses in spelling and punctuation. If the faults are too significant, or too common, the marker might get annoyed. That's not a good thing, as annoyed markers give fewer marks, but spelling and punctuation have to be really bad to make a script impossible to mark.

Similarly, these exams are not a test of your handwriting. I sometimes have to mark work from students with poor handwriting but, once again, it has to be *really* bad to make the work unreadable. Normally, writing in capital letters can solve such problems. Yes, it takes much longer, but it's far better to produce ten legible sides of work than twenty illegible ones. If you (and your friends – ask them) think you're writing is illegible, start writing in capitals *now* and practise every day between now and your next exam.

So, to summarise; learn to write again. Think carefully about each of your sentences, and try to add value in each one. Group your sentences into paragraphs, and try to build a great argument in each one. And don't worry too much about spelling, punctuation, and handwriting.

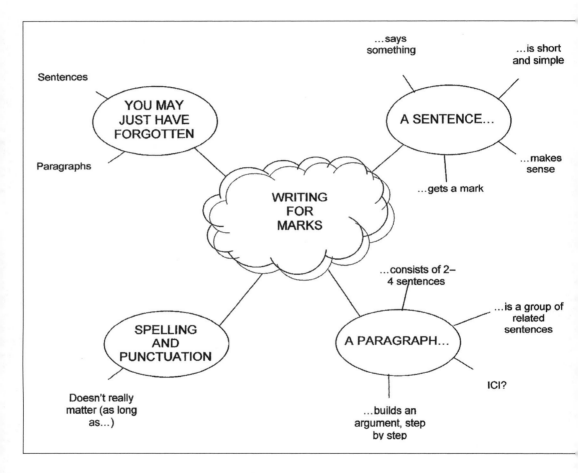

Marker-friendly layout 11

11 Marker-friendly layout

First impressions are really important in exams. I don't mean that you should wear that extra-special Hawaiian shirt, or get your hair done, but that the way your work looks on the page will have some indirect effect on how many marks you earn, Markers, just like the rest of us, are impressed by good presentation and disappointed if it's poor. And a 'disappointed' marker doesn't give as many marks as an 'impressed' one!

The other reason why layout is so important is the nature of the job the markers have to do. CIMA carefully control the scripts to ensure that the standard of marking doesn't slip. Each marker will see a lot of scripts. What each marker wants is to be able to make the decision whether the script is of a 'pass' or 'fail' standard as easily as possible. If you can give them a script that's easy to mark, they'll be happy. If the script is messy, and difficult to mark, they won't be. Happy markers, of course, give more marks.

So just how important is layout and presentation? Some years ago I decided to do 'an experiment' to find out, and the answers surprised even me. I paid some students to sit an exam, then paid them again to sit it again. The first time they sat the exam, they used all the layout and presentation skills that I had taught them. The second time, they just copied out their answers in 'lousy' layout – exactly the same content, just different layout. Then I sent the two groups of exam scripts to the same marker, three months apart.

The first set of results, for the 'good' scripts, was fairly normal. All the students in my test had just passed their CIMA 'finals', so the 85% pass rate wasn't really a surprise. The marks ranged from 34% to 78%, and the average was about 62%.

The second set of results, three months later and for the 'bad' scripts was a lot worse. Several students who'd passed the first exam had failed this one (with exactly the same content in their answers, remember) and the average mark had gone down by 8%, as had the highest and lowest marks. One poor student had passed the first exam with a mark of 72%, but failed the second one with a mark of 40%! That's a difference of 32% (for the same answers, remember) but then, the student did have really poor handwriting.

TOP MARKS FOR PRESENTATION.

So, what's good layout worth to you in the exam? That depends. If the exam is very numerical, or has a lot of OT questions, probably not that much. If the exam is mainly 'written' questions, possibly 10 marks for the 'average' student, and a lot more if your handwriting isn't that great. Is it worth having ten or more marks for a few minutes spent on presentation? I think so.

So what, exactly, is 'best practice' when it comes to laying out your exam script? Well, I think there are six areas where most students could (and should) improve the look of their answers:

- Headings and sub-headings: As a 'route-map' to help the marker navigate through your script, headings, and sub-headings are invaluable. Each requirement that you attempt should have a heading, to let the marker know what topic you're writing about. Under that heading, you should give a sub-heading for each task that you attempt. For example, if the question asks you to 'discuss the value of having a mission statement', your heading should be 'mission statements', and your sub-headings 'advantages', 'disadvantages', and 'conclusion'.
- Paragraphs: We've already talked about the use of paragraphs in the previous chapter. Each point or argument that you make should have its own paragraph of two to four sentences.

- White space: Leave gaps between your paragraphs and answers. A couple of lines between each paragraph, half a side between each task and requirement, and a whole side (or most of one) between questions. White space between paragraphs is nice, as it shows very clearly how much you've written on each point. It also 'frames' your answer, and makes it look much more professional. Big gaps between tasks, requirements, and questions are really useful if you find that you want to add another point without having to 'squeeze it in'.

- Bullets and numbering: None of the examiners like the idea of 'bullet points' if each point is a word or a phrase. That's not what I mean by a bullet point. I mean a series of paragraph-length points with a bullet in front of each of them. If you use bullet points this way, your points are long enough to get good marks, but the marker can also see immediately how many points there are. That's important to the marker, as the marking guide normally says '*x* points at up to *y* marks each'. Numbered points should be used wherever the examiner has asked for a specific number of responses, for example 'explain *five* advantages of...'. By numbering your points, the marker can see right away whether you've done what you were asked to.

- Selective highlighting or underlining: What the marker really wants to do is to mark quickly. If you can, highlight or underline *a single word or short phrase* in each paragraph, that clearly describes the point or argument that you're making. What you're doing is inviting the marker to give you some marks more quickly than they could if they had to (or chose to) read every word that you've written.

- Pro-formas, layouts, labels, and workings: If you have calculations in the exam, it's really important that your layout is perfect. Badly laid out calculations are a nightmare to mark. If you're producing an accounting statement (like an income statement or balance sheet) make sure that you use the 'approved' pro-forma. Lay out your page(s) *before* you do any of the calculations, then just feed in the numbers as you calculate them. Cross-reference any calculated numbers to the appropriate working, so you can be sure to get 'part marks' if you make a stupid mistake. If you're doing a complex calculation you should decide, before you even start the calculation, how you want your finished answer to look. Start your answer by laying out the format of your answer, then do each of the appropriate calculations below the format and cross-reference each of the workings. And always, *always* label the stages in a complex calculation, so the marker can work out what you're trying to do.

Just so you can see an example of all (or most) of these rules in practice, I've included an examiner's suggested answer in Appendix I. Look at it now, and re-read the advice in the previous list of points. The only things you won't find are the use of big gaps between requirements (it's a waste of paper) and selective underlining or highlighting (as I *want* you to read all of it)!

Perhaps the most important thing about clear, professional layout is that marginal scripts will pass. If, for example, the marker gives you 47 or 48 marks, they have to make a decision whether, on balance, you deserve to pass. If they think you do deserve to pass, they're allowed to mark your script up to 50. What will make them change their mind, and let you pass? If the script looks professional.

So, you need to change the way you lay out your written work. Make your 'wordy' answers look like they've come out of a word processing package, and your 'numbers' look like they came out of a spreadsheet package. Smarter scripts are more likely to pass.

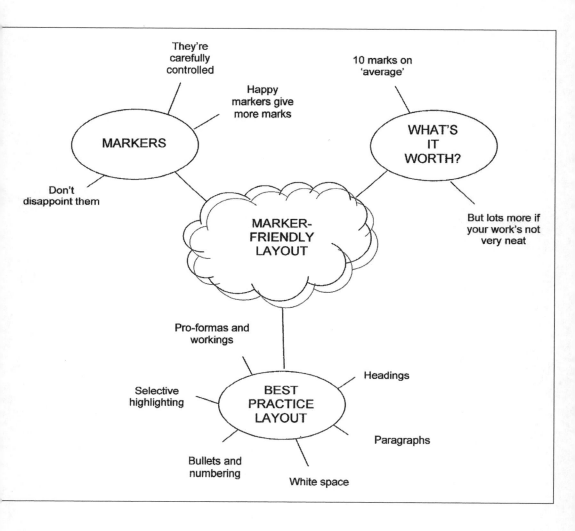

Exit strategy 12

12 Exit strategy

What do you do, in the exam room, if you've finished all the questions that you need to do? Before leaving you should:

- re-read the instructions on the front of the exam paper about how many questions you need to answer, and checked that you've done just that,
- re-read each of the questions you've answered, and asked yourself 'did I actually answer that question, or something slightly (or very) different?', and fix any problems,
- re-read each of your answers and made sure that you can't possibly earn more marks on any of them, and
- made sure that you've completed the information on the front of your script booklet(s).

Once you've done all of these things, you can leave. However, you're one of the lucky few. Most CIMA exam candidates are still furiously writing at the end of the exam. So what do you do if you *haven't* finished?

Well, the best advice I can give you is 'don't get in that position in the first place'. Ideally, you need to manage your time in the exam so that whatever you're planning to do can be done in the available time. This, of course, takes lots of discipline, and also assumes that you have just enough to say to fill the time. No, you're right, it's never going to happen!

If you realise, let's say half an hour before the end of the exam, that you're just not going to finish, you need to implement your 'exit strategy'. That means planning to *not* be able to finish your answers. This is how a possible exit strategy might work:

- When you realise that there's thirty minutes to go, and there's not going to be enough time for you to finish all your answers, stop writing.

- Make sure that you've done answer plans for all the remaining questions. If your time management goes horribly wrong, the marker will mark your answer plan(s), but don't expect to get as many marks as you would for 'full' answers.
- Look at how many points you've still got to write about. Check how many minutes there are until the end of the exam. Work out how many minutes per point that is.
- Start to write your points more briefly than you normally would. That might mean using fewer sentences in each paragraph, or maybe even single sentence bullet points. Try to avoid single word answer and short phrases, as they seldom get any marks at all.
- If you still don't finish, simply write 'see answer plan' as the last thing in your answer, and hope for the best!

Remember, the markers really do want you to pass, so make it easy for them. Don't just stop writing in the middle of an answer, because that just looks unprofessional.

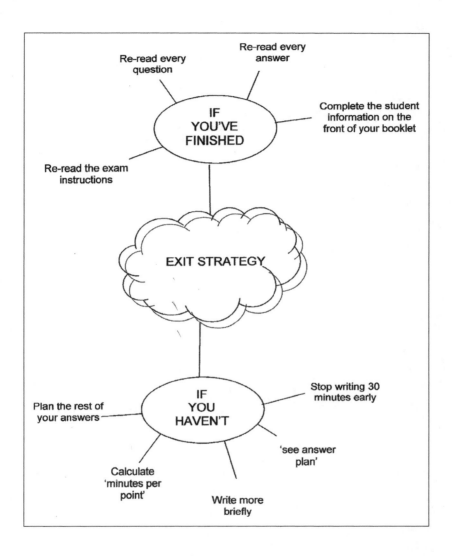

Summary **13**

13 Summary

The whole of this book is full of guidance that can help to improve your chances of passing your CIMA exams. I can't *guarantee* that you'll pass but, if you follow my advice and do a fair bit of work, you should stand the very best chance of passing. My approach to study, revision, and exam technique is all about focusing on the objective – passing the exams. If a technique seems to work, but I can't see how it might increase your chances of passing, I'm not interested.

Although passing your CIMA exams is really important, even important enough for me to write this book about it, it's not *that* important in comparison to family and friends. Don't let your CIMA exams rule your life. Manage your stress levels, and talk to people if the pressure starts to get too much. Of course, the very best way to prevent your CIMA exams taking over your life is to pass them first time! Good luck.

If you have feedback for the author, or any study or exam techniques that have worked for you, he can be contacted at david@cimaguru.com.

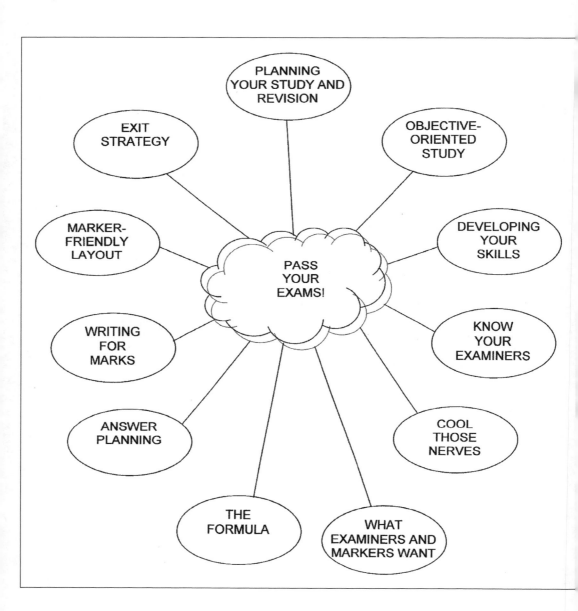

Appendices

Appendix A – The meanings of verbs

The following is based on my article that first appeared in Financial Management magazine in July/August 2005, and is reproduced here with permission.

Introduction

If you look at the post-exam guides published after each exam sitting, there are a number of consistent themes that crop up in almost every one. The one single most common complaint of examiners is 'students just don't answer the question', but there's a whole range of different ways of not answering a question...

- Many students go into the exam determined to prove how much they've learned, and use the questions as an excuse to do just that, regurgitating learned material, and ignoring the question.
- Others answer part of the question, ignoring the fact that the examiner may have required several things to be done in order to get full marks.
- Some even answer the question they hoped would be there, rather than the one that actually is.

Doing any of these things is likely to make it very difficult to pass an exam, but I'm not going to talk about them here. Instead, I'm going to look at one of the most common mistakes that can lead to getting a poor mark in a question– ignoring or misinterpreting the verb. Firstly, let's look at verbs in the syllabus...

The syllabus

Each section within the syllabus contains a series of learning outcomes. Each group of learning outcomes is prefaced with the comment 'On completion of their studies, students should be able to:'. What this means is very clear– these are the things that you might be asked to do *in the exam*. If there isn't a learning outcome, there can't be a question in the exam, because nobody warned

Learning Objectives	Verbs Used	Definition
1 Knowledge *What you are expected to know.*	List State Define	Make a list of Express, fully or clearly, the detail of/facts of Gives the exact meaning of
2 Comprehension *What you are expected to understand.*	Describe Distinguish Explain Identify Illustrate	Communicate the key features of Highlight the differences between Make clear or intelligible/State the meaning of Recognise, establish or select after consideration Use an example to describe or explain something
3 Application *How you are expected to apply your knowledge.*	Apply Calculate/compute Demonstrate Prepare Reconcile Solve Tabulate	Put to practical use Ascertain or reckon mathematically Prove with certainty or to exhibit by practical means Make or get ready for use Make or prove consistent/compatible Find an answer to Arrange in a table
4 Analysis *How you are expected to analyse the detail of what you have learned.*	Analyse Categorise Compare and contrast Construct Discuss Interpret Produce	Examine in detail the structure of Place into a defined class or division Show the similarities and/or defferences between Build up or compile Examine in detail by argument Translate into intelligible or familiar terms Create or bring into existence
5 Evaluation *How you are expected to use your learning to evaluate, make decisions or recommendations.*	Advise Evaluate Recommend	Counsel, inform or notify Appraise or assess the value of Advise on a course of action

Figure 1
The CIMA verb hierarchy

you to be able to do anything else. But the learning outcomes do something else as well– they set an upper limit in the skill level for that area of the syllabus. Let me explain…

Every learning outcome uses a verb, or verbs, from the approved hierarchy published with the syllabus (see Figure 1). This hierarchy gives a brief definition for each verb, but also ranks it in one of five levels. Although the hierarchy is upside-down, it should be obvious that the 'level 5' verbs are a lot more difficult to do than those at 'level 1'. The hierarchy is also meant to be progressive so, as you learn, you work your way 'up' the hierarchy (from level 1 to wherever), increasing your skill level as you go. Why do I say 'to wherever'? Because there is no need to go further than the verb used in the appropriate learning outcome. Let me demonstrate…

Illustration A

In section A of the syllabus for paper P7 (Financial Accounting and Tax Principles) you will find the learning outcome *'explain the difference in principle between tax avoidance and tax evasion'.* The verb *'explain'* is at 'level 2' in the verb hierarchy, so there is no point developing skills relating to this topic (tax avoidance and evasion) that use higher level verbs, as you haven't been asked to do that. Despite the fact that it might be fun to learn how to *advise* an organisation how to evade tax, the syllabus simply does not require you to do so. Apart from being unethical, 'advise' is a level 5 verb. The learning outcome said 'explain', so you only need to be able to demonstrate level 1 and 2 skills in relation to this topic.

The most 'difficult' question that could be set on this topic might be something like *'Distinguish between tax avoidance and tax evasion. Illustrate your answer with appropriate examples. (12 marks)'*

Verbs in exam questions

Just before we leave this illustration, read that question again. Do you notice how the question has two verbs? They both come from level 2 of the hierarchy, so they are covered by the learning outcome, but the examiner has asked you to do *two* specific things. Earlier I said that a lot of students only answer part of the question. That doesn't necessarily mean doing part (a) and ignoring part (b). If the P7 examiner had set the question in illustration A, the marks available for answering that question would be split between the two things that are required in order to answer it. In other words, if you only do the 'distinguish' and not the 'illustrate', you aren't answering the whole question and you can't get full marks. It may well be that there are 6 marks available for the differences between tax evasion and tax avoidance, and a further 6 for relevant examples. Providing only a series of differences, however well you do it, can only get 6 out of 12. If you don't attempt each verb, you aren't answering the whole question.

Hopefully you now see how the position of the verb used in the learning outcome limits the skill level that you need to develop. We've also seen how multiple verbs in an exam question should lead to multiple parts in your answer to it. Let's now look at the range of questions that can be set on an individual learning outcome.

Illustration B

For this illustration I'm going to use a learning outcome from section C of paper P1.

The syllabus says:
> (vi) *'Evaluate and apply alternative approaches to budgeting'.*

The first thing to note is that there are two verbs in this learning outcome; *evaluate* is a level 5 verb, and *apply* comes from level 3. In actual fact, the second verb is unnecessary, as we'll see, but it does serve to reinforce the practical nature of the learning outcome. Given this learning outcome, what can the examiner ask you to do in the exam? Well, pretty much anything, actually! Given the level 5 verb, the examiner is free to use any of the verbs from any level of the hierarchy. This is a really important point – examiners can use verbs from levels *lower* than the learning outcome, but *not higher*. Thus, any of the following questions (and many more), each perfectly valid and *at a different level in the verb hierarchy*, might be asked in paper P1:

Level 1 –   List four alternatives to the traditional 'fixed' approach to budgeting that might be used by an organisation in a dynamic business environment.

Level 2 –   Explain what is meant by the term 'zero-based budgeting'.

Level 3 –   Prepare a flexed budget for X plc, for months 6 to 12, based on the information provided.

Level 4 –   Compare and contrast the use of a rolling budget with the use of a flexible budget, in X plc.

Level 5 –   Advise X plc whether the use of activity-based budgeting would benefit the organisation in its current business environment.

Now we've seen how a whole range of different questions can be asked, each relating to the same learning outcome. We'll come back to this illustration later, when we look at how to earn good marks for a question based on this learning outcome. In the meantime, the next step is to discuss the general principles of how to go about answering a question, depending on the verb used...

Doing it right

Each of the verbs in the hierarchy implies a different approach to be taken, when answering a question that uses that verb. In some cases, the approach is obvious from the definition of the verb, in others it is less so. Let me attempt to clarify the approach that you should take in each case...

Illustration C

- List – As it says, just provide a list. Each of the items on your list should be expressed in terms of a full sentence, for clarity, but there's no need to go any further than that.
- State – Again, pretty obvious. Just say what you need to say in a fairly concise manner. No need to explain or clarify, unless you think that what you've written isn't clear.
- Define – This is really asking for a dictionary or textbook definition, but your own words can be used instead. Asking you to define something is simply a test of memory– a pretty low level skill – but if you use your own words you're actually doing 'describe' or 'explain', which is fine.
- Describe – A straightforward 'what it is' statement. Think of it as the next step on from 'list' or 'state'. However, you might need a short paragraph, rather than a single sentence, depending on how complex or technical the issues are.
- Distinguish – Two or more lists. You can only distinguish *between* things, so there need to be two or more things given in the question. The trick here is only to list the features of each of the things that make them *different* from each other.
- Explain – A tricky one. Quite often examiners ask you to explain something, but get a description instead. Think of it this way – if you are asked to describe a dog, it's easy: Furry animal, four legs, goes 'woof'. Now *explain* a dog. See what I mean? You need more guidance as to what approach to take, or you need to decide on your own approach. It's not possible to explain *what* a dog is, but it's easy to explain *why* people keep dogs as pets, or *how* a dog may be trained. If you're asked to explain something, use a paragraph: Write a sentence that makes your point, then write another to explain why the first sentence is so, or the consequences of the first sentence. If your point still isn't clear, write a third sentence that makes it clearer.
- Identify – To do this, it's really necessary to have a scenario. It's not really application of your knowledge, but more a selective use of it. Think of 'identify' as being like 'explain *in this situation...*'. Go through what you've learned, and pick out only the bits that apply to the situation described in the question.
- Illustrate – Easy. Give an example. If there's a scenario, give a relevant example. If not, pick whichever you like. Alternatively, you could draw a picture (we call them 'diagrams') or do a quick calculation by way of illustration (as in 'explain and illustrate what is meant by an adverse variance').

- Apply – This verb is used quite a bit in the learning outcomes, but rarely in exam questions. In a learning outcome it means that you'll have to do it for real, not just talk about it in theory. In the exam, you're more likely to be given a different (and more specific) verb from level 3.
- Calculate/compute – Obvious. Do the math.
- Demonstrate – A tough one. You need to prove something to be true, beyond any doubt, or show that it applies in the situation described, by giving evidence. This verb is most likely to be used in situations where there is one correct answer, rather than where you are expressing an opinion. Think of it as an explanation with an illustration.
- Prepare – For this verb to be used, there has to be a fair amount of (often numerical) data in the question. You take the relevant data, process it (perhaps by calculation, but often just by re-arranging it), then provide it in a particular format. The best example I can think of is 'Prepare a balance sheet from the trial balance provided…'.
- Reconcile – Another numerical one, this time asking you to prove that two things (often the results of calculations) are the same as, or are consistent with, one another. Think about reconciling an Income Statement to two Balance Sheets.
- Solve – Again, generally, calculating an answer to something. Literally, providing a solution. However, whereas 'calculate' normally tells you *how* to do something, 'solve' may leave *you* to choose the most appropriate method.
- Tabulate – Obvious. Produce a two-dimensional table of results.
- Analyse – Now we're starting to get into the really difficult stuff. This is asking for a series of detailed explanations, often opinions rather than facts, each with an illustration (if appropriate). Think about 'analyse the published accounts…': Calculate some ratios, explain what you think they mean, relate them to each other, relate them to the context of the question. Alternatively, what about 'analyse the variances…'? The same set of steps? I think so.
- Categorise – A number of lists, with an explanation after each item saying why you put it in that particular list and not one of the others.
- Compare and contrast – Fairly obviously an explanation of the similarities and differences between two (or more) things. Compare and contrast a dog and a cat? They're both furry animals, but one goes 'woof' and the other 'miaow'.
- Construct – Like 'prepare', but possibly with an explanation as to why you put things where you did.
- Discuss – This is a tricky one. In order to discuss something, there needs to be an 'argument'. In other words, you need two or more differing or

opposing viewpoints. Also, any discussion should, if possible, end in a conclusion. Think about; advantages, disadvantages, conclusion. Or; reasons why, reasons why not, conclusion. Or; maybe this, maybe that, conclusion. Can you 'discuss' one viewpoint? Sure. Examiners often ask you to 'discuss the advantages of...'. Does that mean you have to do the disadvantages as well? No. Simply go through the advantages, saying whether they apply in this situation, or whether they're each a major advantage or a relatively minor one.

- Interpret – Literally, translating from one form of words to another, where the latter is more understandable than the former. 'Interpret' is often the second stage of 'analyse'. Think about variances again. In order to produce a 'variance analysis', first you calculate the variances, then you interpret them. Got it?

- Produce – This is really creative stuff. You start with very little (or nothing), and end up with the finished article. How about, given two Balance Sheets and an Income Statement, 'produce a Cash Flow Statement...'? Or, what about 'produce a report...'?

- Advise – Tell them what you think they could, or should, do. Construct a good, comprehensive, argument that leads to one or more options for the owners or managers (normally) to consider pursuing. An *evaluate* with a *recommend*– it doesn't get any more difficult than this. Why is 'advise' not last on the list (at the 'top' of the hierarchy)? I assume because, within each 'level', the verbs are listed alphabetically. Except for 'define', which isn't, but I think that's probably a mistake!

- Evaluate – The second of our 'top level' verbs, and another tricky one. Think of *evaluate* as a higher level *discuss*. It might mean calculations, but it might not. You can say how valuable something is in qualitative terms, as well as monetary. This is easier to illustrate than to explain, so I'll give an example later (see Illustration D).

- Recommend – Just that. Tell them what to do. Often, when recommend is used in an exam question, it's the last requirement. Unless you're specifically asked to, there's no need to evaluate before you recommend. Quite often, the evaluation is an earlier part of the same question. If there are three requirements (a, b, and c), you might find that part (a) says 'explain' or 'identify', part (b) says 'discuss' or 'evaluate', and part (c) says 'recommend'. Are these the three stages of an 'advise' answer? I think so.

Hopefully it's now fairly clear what each verb means and, with the possible exception of 'evaluate', how to do exactly what you're told to in any exam question. You may have noticed, by the way, that several of the 'higher level' verbs imply a series of steps that often encompass verbs from lower levels. Let's have a look at that in more detail, and work out just how to 'evaluate'…

Step by step towards a high level verb

Often, and particularly at the Strategic Level or in the TOPCIMA case study, you'll be given a single requirement that's worth quite a lot of marks. This can look very daunting, but you can make life so much easier for yourself if you remember the verb hierarchy. Rather than seeing it as one big question, break it down into a series of smaller ones that work progressively up the levels of the hierarchy. Let me explain…

Illustration D

Let's assume that you're in your Paper P1 exam, and the question has a scenario describing an organisation called X plc. From the scenario, it's obvious that X plc only does boring, traditional, annual budgets. Part (a) of the question asked you to identify the weaknesses of this approach to budgeting (for 6 marks), and you've done that. It's part (b) that scares you…

(b) Evaluate two alternative approaches to budgeting that could be used by X plc.(14 marks)

This question refers to the learning outcome used in illustration B. If it's a while since you looked at it, re-read that illustration now.

Notice that the examiner has already made life easier for you, by limiting you to *two* alternatives. This means that some of the 14 marks will be available for each of the alternatives, and also that there's no point considering more than two. Which two will you consider? Well, it has to be two that are appropriate (in this case they should remove some or all of the weaknesses you identified in part a), and they have to be ones that you feel confident writing about. There's not much point picking an approach to budgeting about which you know nothing!

OK. Let's break down the question using the verb hierarchy…

Step 1

For each of the two alternative approaches to budgeting that we have *identified* as being relevant, let's begin by briefly *describing* what they are, and *explaining* how they work. Let's assume that this gets us 2 marks for each– 4 down, 10 to go.

Step 2

For each of the two approaches, let's now *discuss* the extent to which each of them eliminates the weaknesses identified in part (a), *illustrating* by means of examples from the scenario. Because the skill level is higher, and we've had to do two verbs, let's assume 4 marks each – 12 down, 2 to go.

Step 3

Finally, let's conclude which of the two is likely to give the most benefit to X plc, again *illustrating* by means of an example, or simply by summarising which one negates more of the weaknesses mentioned in part (a). Last 2 marks earned – all 14 in the bag!

Using this approach, it's easy to see how even the most 'difficult' question, with a high level verb, can be broken down into a series of more doable stages by using the verb hierarchy. All you need to do now is practise using this approach on a few questions.

Conclusion

Hopefully, having read and understood this article, you should now be able to:

- Interpret more clearly what the syllabus might require you to be able to do in the exam.
- Analyse the learning outcomes, to identify what you won't be asked to do in the exam.
- Produce answers that take the right approach to answering each exam question, depending on which verb or verbs it uses.
- Analyse a difficult question with a high level verb, and break it down into a series of straightforward steps, each of which uses a verb or verbs from a lower level of the hierarchy, to earn marks progressively.

Appendix B – Post-exam guide extract: Paper P6, November 2005

Paper 6 – Management Accouting Business Strategy
Post Exam Guide
November 2005 Examination

SECTION B – 50 MARKS
ANSWER *TWO* QUESTIONS FROM FOUR

Question 2*(a)*

Evaluate whether the 222 Organisation might gain a competitive advantage as a result of being based in Jurania.
(13 marks)

Rationale

This is a more difficult question than previously asked on this topic (Porter's diamond) as it only requires application.

Suggested Approach

Each aspect of the diamond could be related to specific facts in the scenario, to support the required evaluation. As an evaluation was required, some opinions as to the relative significance of each point were hoped for.

Marking Guide

	Marks
Porter's diamond; overview and diagram (if provided), up to	2
Demand condtions, up to	3
Factor conditions, up to	3
Firm strategy, structure and rivalry, up to	3
Related and supporting industries, up to	3
Conclusion, if given	2
Maximum marks awarded	**13**

Examiner's Comments

This question was answered reasonably well by some candidates. Others, however, displayed weak understanding of the theory and an inability to spot 'clues' in the scenario relating to each aspect of the diamond. Very few marks were awarded to theoretical discussions of the diamond, nor was it possible to earn a pass mark without mentioning or applying the model.

Common Errors
- Poor understanding
- No application to the facts given
- Just an explanation, rather than an evaluation
- No mention of Porter's diamond at all

Appendix C – Sample contexts

Use these as a starter for practising application of theoretical models and concepts. Write more contexts of your own, for further practice...

A is a multinational car manufacturer. It employs 8,000 staff in three large factories and a headquarters building. The factories are each in a different European country, and the Headquarters is adjacent to one of the factories. A sells its products through a large number of franchised retail outlets, none of which is owned by A. A is listed on the stock exchange of the European country in which it has its headquarters.

B is a small charity, specialising in helping homeless people. B has only 35 employees, several of whom are part time. B relies on a very large number of voluntary staff to carry out its activities. B is funded by a combination of government grants and donations. Donors are ordinary individuals, many of whom donate a small percentage of their monthly income, or large corporations, which receive tax benefits on their donations.

C&D is a large public relations practice. It is owned by the eight partners of the firm, each of whom is liable for a share of the firm's liabilities. The firm employs about fifty staff, and has modern offices in a busy city. The clients of C&D are large, well-known organisations. C&D has a reputation for very high levels of customer service and, in return, charges relatively high fees for its services.

E is a government department, responsible for the provision of transport services in a small African country. E employs 2,000 staff in a large office building in the capital city. E is funded by the central treasury function of the government, and is not permitted to exceed its budgeted expenditure levels. For each of the last five years, E has received the same expenditure budget, despite annual inflation rates of between two and five per cent.

Appendix D – Sample mind map

The following mind map illustrates how the technique can be used to produce revision notes. This mind map is for the learning outcome *'identify methods of conducting research and gathering data as part of the managerial process'*, from Section C of the syllabus for Paper P5.

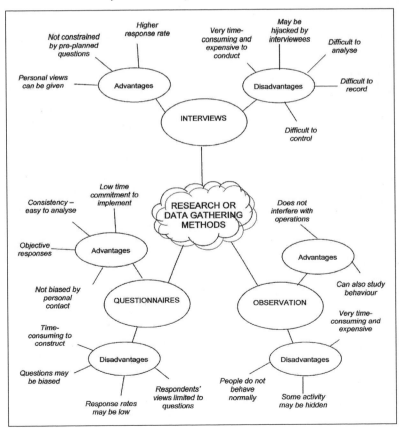

Appendix E – Paper P6, November 2005, question 3

Question Three

C is a large multinational car manufacturer. It has factories in five countries and sells its products through networks of independent dealerships throughout the world. As part of its strategy of reducing unit costs and improving quality, C has entered into a number of 'sole supplier' agreements. This means that, on a worldwide basis, C buys all of its requirement for a specific material or component from a single supplier organisation. Such contracts are normally for a five year period.

S is a specialist manufacturer of safety equipment. It has recently been invited, by C, to submit a tender to supply all of the 'airbag' safety devices to be installed in C's cars. This will be the biggest order for which S has ever tendered and, if won, would require a two hundred per cent increase in production capacity (that is, to three times its present scale) for S. In return for this large order, S would have to agree to deliver the required parts to each C factory twice a day. Any failure to deliver on time would lead to S being liable for the cost of lost production.

As part of the contract, C would allow S access to its extranet. This would mean that S was able to see C's forecast production schedules on a real-time basis. C maintains detailed forecasts of the number of each model of car being produced in each factory. This information is available on an hour-by-hour basis for the next month, on a day-by-day basis for the following five months, and a week-by-week basis for the subsequent 18 months. This means that S would be able to view detailed production forecasts for a two year period. The extranet also has a 'virtual trading room' where suppliers bid for new contracts. It also contains a lot of car industry information, some of which is not available to organisations that do not supply C.

Required:

(a) Discuss the advantages and disadvantages, to S, of the sole supplier arrangement described.

(15 marks)

(b) Evaluate the benefits, to S, of access to the C extranet.

(10 marks)

(Total for Question Three = 25 marks)

Appendix F – Sample answer plan 1 – short answer format

Question Two

S & C is a medium-sized firm that is experiencing rapid growth evidenced by increased turnover.

It has been able to develop a range of new consultancy and specialist business advisory services that it offers to its growing customer base. To cope with these developments several organisation-wide initiatives have been launched over the past two years.

The existing financial systems are struggling to cope with these developments, but replacement software is due to be installed within the next six months. The new system was justified partly because it could reduce costs although precise details have not been given.

The application software does not fit existing business processes exactly. However, it has the clear advantage of giving S & C access to an industry best practice system and is identical to that used by all its main competitors and some of its clients.

A three-person project steering group has recommended that a phased approach to introduction should be used and has undertaken most of the project planning. A programme of events for implementing the system has been agreed but is not yet fully operational. This group has not met for a while because the designated project manager has been absent from work through illness.

You are Head of S & C's Central Support Unit. You also serve on the project steering group. A partners' meeting is due to take place soon. The firm's senior partner has asked you to prepare a PowerPoint presentation to other partners on implementation issues. You understand that partners are conscious that system implementation represents a form of further organisational change. They are asking questions about the approach that will be taken to the introduction of the new system, likely changes to practices, critical areas for success, system testing, support after implementation, system effectiveness, etc.

Required:

You are required to produce **outline notes** that will support your eventual PowerPoint presentation. These notes should:

(a) Discuss the options to overcome the fact that the software does not fit existing business processes exactly.

(5 marks)

(b) Explain why a phased approach to introducing the system is, in this case, more suitable than a direct 'big bang' approach.

(5 marks)

(c) Discuss the ways in which particular individuals and groups within S & C are important for implementation to succeed.

(5 marks)

(d) Explain how users should be involved in the implementation phase of the project.

(5 marks)

(e) Describe the training that should be given to targeted groups within S & C.

(5 marks)

(f) Explain the aims of a post-implementation review.

(5 marks)

(Total for Question Two = 30 marks)

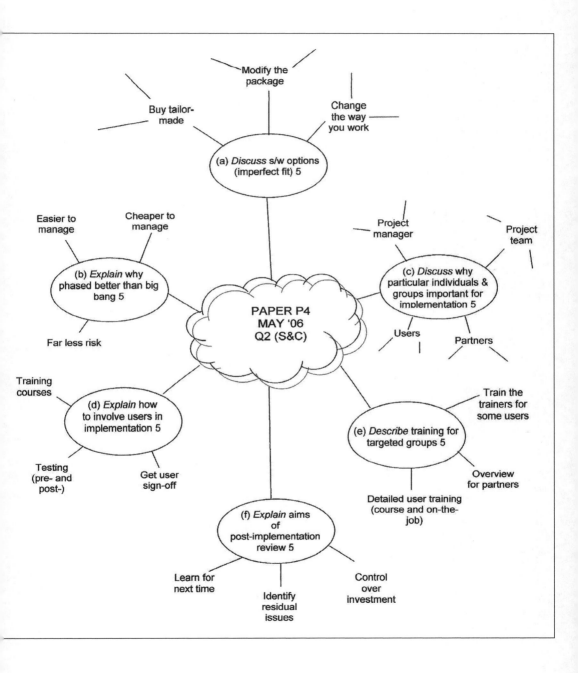

Appendix G – Sample answer plan 2 – calculate and explain format

Question Three

M plc designs, manufactures, and assembles furniture. The furniture is for home use and therefore varies considerably in size, complexity, and value. One of the departments in the company is the Assembly Department. This department is labour intensive; the workers travel to various locations to assemble and fit the furniture using the packs of finished timbers that have been sent to them.

Budgets are set centrally and they are then given to the managers of the various departments who then have the responsibility of achieving their respective targets. Actual costs are compared against the budgets and the managers are then asked to comment on the budgetary control statement. The statement for April for the Assembly Department is shown below.

	Budget	Actual	Variance	
Assembly labour hours	6,400	7,140		
	$	$	$	
Assembly labour	51,970	58,227	6,257	Adverse
Furniture packs	224,000	205,000	19,000	Favourable
Other materials	23,040	24,100	1,060	Adverse
Overheads	62,060	112,340	50,280	Adverse
Total	361,070	399,667	38,597	Adverse

Note: the costs shown are for assembling and fitting the furniture (they do not include time spent travelling to jobs and the related costs). The hours worked by the Manager are not included in the figure given for the assembly labour hours.

The Manager of the Assembly Department is new to the job and has very little previous experience of working with budgets but he does have many years' experience as a supervisor in assembly departments. Based on that experience he was sure that the department had performed well. He has asked for your help in replying to a memo he has just received asking him to 'explain the serious overspending in his department'. He has sent you some additional information about the budget:

1. The budgeted and actual assembly labour costs include the fixed salary of $2,050 for the Manager of the Assembly Department. All of the other labour is paid for the hours they work.
2. The cost of furniture packs and other materials is assumed by the central finance office of M plc to vary in proportion to the number of assembly labour hours worked.
3. The budgeted overhead costs are made up of three elements: a fixed cost of $9,000 for services from central headquarters, a stepped fixed cost which changes when the assembly hours exceed 7,000 hours, and some variable overheads. The variable overheads are assumed to vary in proportion to the number of assembly labour hours. Working papers for the budget showed the impact on the overhead costs of differing amounts of assembly labour hours:

Assembly labour hours	5,000	7,500	10,000
Overhead costs	$54,500	$76,500	$90,000

The actual fixed costs for April were as budgeted.

Required:

(a) Prepare, using the additional information that the Manager of the Assembly Department has given you, a budgetary control statement that would be more helpful to him.

(7 marks)

(b)

(i) Discuss the differences between **the format of the statement** that you have produced and that supplied by M plc.

(4 marks)

(ii) Discuss the assumption made by the central office of M plc that costs vary in proportion to assembly labour hours.

(3 marks)

(c) Discuss whether M plc should change to a system of participative budgeting.

(6 marks)

(Total for Question Three = 20 marks)

(a) Control statement				
	Actual	Budget	Variance	Comments
Xxxxxxxx				
Xxxxxxxx				
Xxxxxxxxxx				
Xxxxxxxxx				
Xxxxxxxxxx				
Xxxxxxxxxxx				

PAPER P1
MAY '06
Q3 (M plc)

Variances –
Better range

(b) *Discuss*
differences between
my format and theirs
4

Level of
analysis –
More
detailed

Assumptions –
More
reasonable

(c) *Discuss*
assumption that costs
vary with labour hours
3

Vary with
what?

Fixed or variable?

(d) *Discuss*
whether M should use
participative budgeting
6

Advantages:
Motivation
Learning

Disadvantages:
Cost
Slack

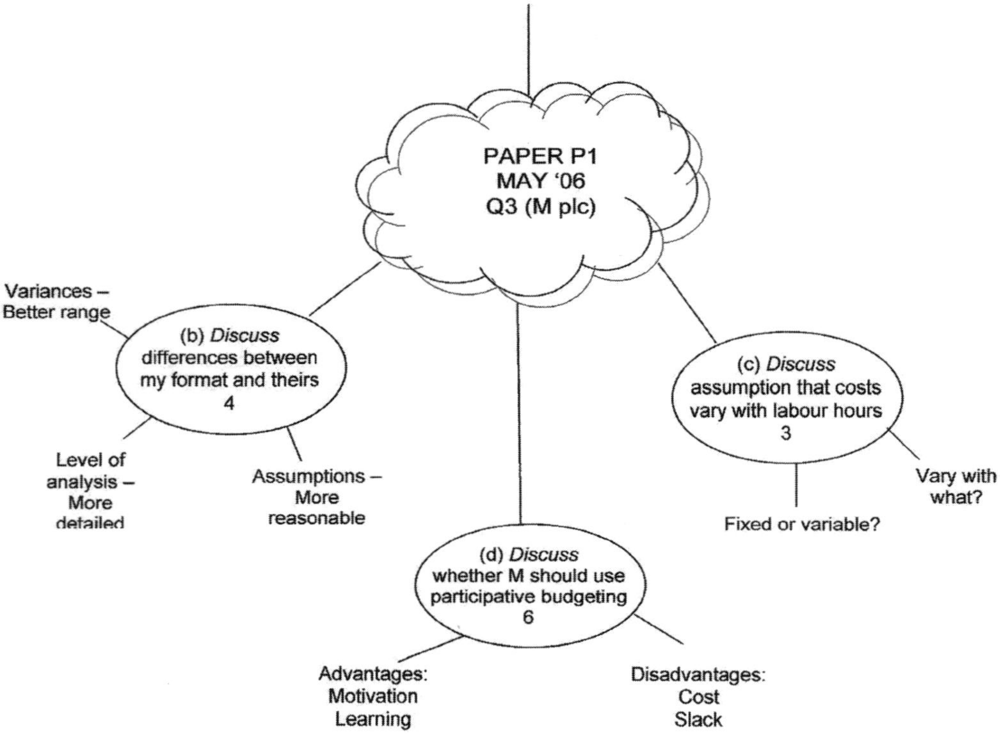

Appendix H – Paper P6, November 2005, suggested answer to question 3

Requirement (a)

The main advantages of the sole supplier agreement to S are as follows:

- Receiving such a contract from a major multinational customer would bring great prestige to S. This may allow it to use the publicity generated to its advantage and it should be able to generate still more business. Winning such a contract implies that S is a high quality, reliable supplier.
- Such a significant contract will allow S to grow its business by two hundred percent. Provided that the terms of the contract are favourable enough, this should lead to a significant improvement in S's profitability. S may also be able to improve margins on its existing business, as a result of economies of scale.
- Having a large, long-term contract will allow S to plan for the future of its business with greater certainty. This will reduce the inherent risk in the business and may also reduce the cost of capital of S. This will further allow S to engage in other developmental strategies without worrying too much about its core business.
- A secondary benefit of the contract to S will be that its employees feel more secure in their jobs. This should lead to improved motivation levels and a subsequent increase in productivity. This may further improve margins, as output increases and costs (such as sickness and absenteeism) reduce.

There are, however, a number of risks to S that may turn out to be disadvantages if not managed effectively:

- Such a significant growth in the business may lead to S 'overtrading'. The consequence of this may be that operational cashflows are insufficient to meet the needs of the business. This will be particularly true if the contract necessitates S undertaking large capital investments. S may need to build a new factory and will almost certainly need a large investment in working capital.
- There is also a credit risk inherent in any large contract. C may have a poor track record in the settlement of payables. It may also believe that S is a 'soft touch' when deciding on credit policies, as S relies on the large contract and is therefore unlikely to complain too much if payments are delayed.
- Having one customer representing a large proportion of turnover is a dangerous situation for S. If C were to become insolvent, the result might be that S also goes out of business. S should look for opportunities to secure other contracts that do not rely on C.
- The 'liquidated damages' payable to C, if S should fail to deliver on time, are likely to be many times higher than the cost of the airbags supplied. The price of a car will be much greater than the cost of an airbag. This may lead to S paying very large penalties for relatively minor delays in supply, so S may find that occasional delays in delivery lead to an erosion of the profit margin on the contract. This risk is much greater because C operates in five countries.
- Having a very large customer gives that customer significant bargaining power. S may find itself under continual pressure to improve quality and decrease price. The contract may also require a large amount of management and administration time, which would further decrease margins.
- There is also significant risk that C may not renew the contract when it expires in five years time. This would leave S with significant surplus capacity and may potentially lead to S becoming unprofitable.
- As C is a multinational, operating in five countries, it may require S to invoice in a currency (or currencies) other than S's own. This would introduce significant foreign exchange risk.

There are significant benefits to S, but it must manage the risks identified above if it is to make significant profit from the contract. A formal risk management strategy should be developed.

Requirement (b)

The main benefits to S of being given access to the C Extranet are as follows:

- The detailed information of C's requirements for the next two years will allow S to plan its production schedules with certainty for a large proportion of its business. This significantly reduces the risk involved in recruiting and training staff and investing in capital equipment. S should try to integrate its production planning system with the information in the C Extranet, thus reducing costs and improving margins.

- The detailed information available for the next month's production will allow S to ensure that deliveries are made on time. This will reduce or eliminate the risk of penalty payments for failure to deliver. It is not clear whether these hour-by-hour requirements can change significantly, so efforts must be made to pursuade C to 'fix' the requirement for at least the first few days.

- S will be able to identify trends in the car industry and, for example, to predict the likely impact of any new technologies. This will further improve planning and may also lead to a potential for competitive advantage (through differentiation) over those of its rivals who do not have access to the Extranet. This advantage would be gained if S was able to exploit trends earlier than its rivals.

- Access to the virtual trading room may give S a 'preferential bidder' status for any new contracts that C offers. This technology vastly reduces the costs of the bid process, so there may be a potential for S to quote lower prices or earn higher margins on future contracts. This, again, is a potential source of competitive advantage (this time through cost leadership).

Access to the C Extranet will provide S with significant benefits. It is difficult to see any disadvantage to S and there is a potential for competitive advantage that may outweigh the risks of the sole supplier agreement discussed above.

Appendix I – Paper P6, May 2006, suggested answer to question 1

Answer to Question One

Requirement (a)

Introduction
The industry of CCC is defined as the specialist sports car industry in Europe. It is analysed below, using the 'five forces' model.

Rivalry
Rivalry looks at the number of organisations, within the industry, supplying similar products to the same customers. It also looks at the extent of competitive activity between those organisations. The major car manufacturers are not rivals, as they cannot supply this type of vehicle. There are only six specialist sports car manufacturers in Europe, and these are all assumed to be rivals. There has historically been little price competition; therefore there has historically been little rivalry. The six appear to have widely differentiated products, and this has led to the current position.

Threat of new entrants
The threat of new entrants is the extent to which the rivals have to divert time and cost to the erection and maintenance of entry barriers. It is assumed that all 6 rivals, in line with CCC, have significant up-front capital costs invested in design, sales promotion, and marketing. This creates a significant barrier to entry. CCC pays high salaries to engender staff loyalty, as must the other rivals to remain competitive, and this creates a further barrier to entry.

Threat of substitutes
A substitute is any product or service that fulfils the same purpose or need. The threat of substitutes is that they will steal away market volume, thus affecting

all rivals equally. Substitutes include other 'vanity' purchases such as yachts, powerboats, expensive holidays, and even private planes. The product made by CCC and its rivals is not really a car, it is a status symbol and an expensive toy. There are many substitutes for the high disposable income of CCC's customers.

Bargaining power of suppliers

An organisation competes with its suppliers for margin, the most common methods of such competition being arguments over cost/price and quality. Most supplies are relatively minor components, such as wheels and tyres, which could probably be sourced from alternative suppliers without any risk. The engine modification only comes from SSS, which is able to dictate terms. It appears that SSS may earn the same profit on an engine as CCC does on a car. CCC cannot switch from SSS, as customers see value added in the use of SSS engines. SSS is not contracted to supply only CCC. This suggests that, in general terms, the bargaining power of suppliers is low. However, the bargaining power of SSS is very high.

Bargaining power of customers

The organisation competes with its customers in the same ways as with its suppliers. Historically these customers have had little bargaining power, due to the differentiation of the various specialist sports cars, but their power is increasing due, perhaps, to the effects of recession. Customers are now negotiating price down and, until they sign a contract, have few switching costs other than loss of prestige.

Conclusion

Competitive forces have increased recently, driving profit margins down from nearly 20% (2002) to 7.5% (2005). This has forced a drastic reduction in the level of dividend paid, and significantly reduced shareholder value.

Requirement (b)

SSS – position and performance

Ratios	Working	SSS	Industry Average
Revenue per employee	1	€306,875	€128,500
Return on revenue (gross)	2	43.1%	
Return on revenue (pre-tax)	3	7.7%	4.3%
ROCE (gross)	4	99.7%	

Ratios	Working	SSS	Industry Average
ROCE (pre-tax)	5	17.9%	11.2%
Dividend cover	6	2.05x	
Profit per employee (gross)	7	€132,125	
Profit per employee (pre-tax)	8, 8a	€23,750	€5,526
Current ratio	9	1.68	
Quick (acid test) ratio	10	0.73	
Non-current assets turnover	11	2.75x	
Inventory days (cost of sales)	12	61	
Receivables days (revenue)	13	22	65
Payables days (cost of sales)	14	64	28

Workings

1 $2,455,000/8 = 306,875$
2 $(2,455 - 1,398)/2,455 = 1,057/2,455 = 43.1\%$
3 $190/2,455 = 7.7\%$
4 $1,057/(100 + 960) = 1,057/1,060 = 99.7\%$
5 $190/1,060 = 17.9\%$
6 $133/65 = 2.05\times$
7 $1,057,000/8 = 132,125$
8 $190,000/8 = 23,750$
8a $128,500 \times 4.3\% = 5,526$
9 $(232 + 146 + 32)/244 = 410/244 = 1.68$
10 $(146 + 32)/244 = 178/244 = 0.73$
11 $2,455/894 = 2.75\times$
12 $(232/1,398) \times 365 = 0.166 \times 365 = 61$
13 $(146/2,455) \times 365 = 0.059 \times 365 = 22$
14 $(244/1,398) \times 365 = 0.175 \times 365 = 64$

Commentary

With revenue per employee of 2.4 times the industry average (and likewise, a pre-tax ROCE of 1.6 times the average), SSS appears either very efficient, or to charge very high prices. It is unlikely that the reason for this high figure is a high degree of automation (resulting in a low headcount) as the nature of SSS's business is labour-intensive. Pre-tax margin of 1.8 times the average seems to point to higher than average prices. Return on capital employed is similarly high, supporting this conclusion.

Just for comparison, CCC has revenue per employee of €39,166 (€11 75M/300), and pre-tax Return on Revenue of 7.5% (compared to SSS – 7.7%). The two companies are, however, in very different business sectors.

It is possible, however, that the pre-tax (after interest) ratios of SSS are all higher than average as a result of the fact that SSS has no debt. Most of the other firms in the industry may be highly geared, thus reducing their pre-tax earnings levels. It has not been possible to calculate operating level ratios for the industry.

A dividend cover of over 2x suggests a reasonably high margin of safety. However, as an owner-managed business, this will be of little importance to the owner. The pre-tax profit per employee, of €23,750, is a very impressive performance. This figure is over four times the average, underlining the apparent efficiency of SSS. Just for comparison, CCC employees each generate only €2,933 pre-tax profit.

While the current and quick ratios appear low, it is not possible to compare these to the industry average, so no conclusions can be drawn. However, it is more likely to be a result of aggressive working capital management (see below) than poor liquidity.

Inventory days of 61 (assumed to consist of raw materials and WIP only, due to the 'to order' nature of SSS's business) are quite high, bearing in mind that CCC supplies the engines. However, SSS may be replacing many engine parts with very expensive alternatives.

The low receivables days of 22, far less than one month, suggests that a large proportion of sales are either paid for in cash or by stage payments. This underlines the significant bargaining power that SSS has over its customers, CCC included. It is not known what payment terms CCC takes from SSS.

The high payables days of 64 suggests that SSS also exerts high bargaining power over its suppliers, though there may be a risk of losing some suppliers as a result of such aggressive credit policies.

Other performance indicators

For SSS to have made its service to CCC a unique selling point of CCC's product is an impressive achievement. It is very easy for the providers of sub-contracted services to remain 'invisible' to the end consumer. This suggests that SSS has invested heavily in the 'pull' marketing (i.e. to the end consumer) of its services. Further evidence of the strong bargaining power of SSS can be seen in its refusal to negotiate on price, or to sign a sole customer agreement with CCC.

Conclusions

SSS appears to be an extremely efficient and successful organisation. Its only one weak point is its aggressive supplier credit policy.

Requirement (c)

Options to defeat SSS

CCC has four options if it wishes to reduce the bargaining power of SSS:

1. *To exert its own bargaining power.* It is not known what percentage of its business SSS does with CCC, but it must be a significant proportion. This should, theoretically, give CCC an opportunity to be more aggressive in negotiating prices and credit terms with SSS. However, this type of approach has already failed, so is unlikely to succeed in the future. It may also result in a worsening relationship between SSS and CCC, and even worse terms. The worst result might be that SSS decides not to supply CCC in future. This would have a disastrous effect on CCC as the SSS-tuned engine is a major USP of its cars.
2. *To avoid dealing with SSS.* CCC could seek an alternative supplier of engine tuning, preferably one with as good a reputation as SSS. However, there would still be significant consequences for CCC, as it would have to invest in developing a new supplier relationship, and in persuading its customers to accept engines that are not prepared by SSS.
3. *To bring tuning services in-house.* This would probably involve recruitment of suitably skilled staff, or possibly 'headhunting' key staff from SSS. In addition to the cost and lead time implications of this strategy, CCC would once again be faced with the problem of persuading its customers to accept cars without SSS tuned engines.
4. *To acquire SSS.* Subject to having funds available, the preferred option would seem to be to acquire SSS. Though this would depend on the willingness of the current owner to sell (but to remain involved), he might be persuaded to take a shareholding in CCC in return for SSS. The price of SSS could be anywhere between € 0.7m and € 1m, (see below), or even more depending

on the view of the owner. The P/E-based valuation uses a P/E ratio that is probably not relevant to a small, private company like SSS. However, it is included here as indicative of a starting point for negotiation.

The biggest benefit to CCC of acquisition, in addition to the removal of SSS's bargaining power, would be the control it would have over the business. CCC could refuse to provide services from SSS to any of CCC's rivals, effectively giving it a monopoly over the services of SSS.

*Note: It is possible to earn full marks for this requirement **without** valuing SSS Valuations:*

Net asset valuation	= 100,000 + 960,000 = **€1.06M**
P/E valuation	= €133,000 × 7.5 = **€1.00M**

Assumption: P/E valuation may be reduced by up to one-third for non-marketability of SSS shares, thus giving a value between about €0.7m and € 1m.